SIGHT**READING**

MASTERY**FOR**GUITAR

Unlimited Reading and Rhythm Exercises in All Keys

JOSEPH**ALEXANDER**

FUNDAMENTAL**CHANGES**

Sight Reading Mastery for Guitar

Unlimited Reading and Rhythm Exercises in All Keys

ISBN: 978-1-78933-044-1

Published by **www.fundamental-changes.com**

www.fundamental-changes.com

Twitter: @guitar_joseph

Over 10,000 fans on Facebook: **FundamentalChangesInGuitar**

Instagram: **FundamentalChanges**

For over 350 Free Guitar Lessons with Videos Check Out

www.fundamental-changes.com

Cover Image Copyright: Can Stock Photo Inc. / CapturedNuance

Other Books from Fundamental Changes

The Complete Guide to Playing Blues Guitar Book One: Rhythm Guitar

The Complete Guide to Playing Blues Guitar Book Two: Melodic Phrasing

The Complete Guide to Playing Blues Guitar Book Three: Beyond Pentatonics

The Complete Guide to Playing Blues Guitar Compilation

The CAGED System and 100 Licks for Blues Guitar

Fundamental Changes in Jazz Guitar: The Major ii V I

Minor ii V Mastery for Jazz Guitar

Jazz Blues Soloing for Guitar

Guitar Scales in Context

Guitar Chords in Context Part One

Jazz Guitar Chord Mastery (Guitar Chords in Context Part Two)

Complete Technique for Modern Guitar

Funk Guitar Mastery

The Complete Technique, Theory and Scales Compilation for Guitar

Sight Reading Mastery for Guitar

Rock Guitar Un-CAGED: The CAGED System and 100 Licks for Rock Guitar

The Practical Guide to Modern Music Theory for Guitarists

Beginner's Guitar Lessons: The Essential Guide

Chord Tone Soloing for Jazz Guitar

Heavy Metal Rhythm Guitar

Heavy Metal Lead Guitar

Exotic Pentatonic Soloing for Guitar

Heavy Metal Rhythm Guitar

Voice Leading Jazz Guitar

The Complete Jazz Soloing Compilation

The Jazz Guitar Chords Compilation

Fingerstyle Blues Guitar

Contents

Introduction

Why sight read?

In a modern world where we have instant access to guitar tablature, YouTube videos, slowdown software, lesson apps and midi, why is there value in learning to read music fluently on our instrument?

There are many reasons, but the truth is that there is no better way to learn and understand your instrument.

As guitarists, we are constantly surrounded by tablature. There is nothing wrong with this at all, but ask yourself, how many other instruments have this system available? Virtually every other musician you will work with in real life will have to read music to some degree. The point is this: if you walk up to a violin player and point anywhere on their instrument, they will instantly know which note you are pointing to.

Violins, violas, cellos and contra bass don't even have frets! These musicians have worked hard to memorise their fretboard and as such have a much deeper understanding of how their instrument functions.

This means that most working musicians know their instrument inside out. As guitarists, we refer to notes as "the 10th fret on the 2nd string". If we're to be taken seriously then we should really be able to just play an 'A'.

Following on from the above, another good reason to know our instrument is simply for the ability to communicate with other musicians. Imagine you're at a band rehearsal and you're trying out a new section. You're the only guitarist and you're asked to play a sequence of notes as a harmony. The keyboard player says, "OK! Play F, C, Bb, A then G." If you don't know your neck then you're going to have to be taught this phrase note by note, slowly, by ear. If you're in a studio, that's exactly the point where you lose the gig.

Often the quickest way to convey a musical idea is to write it down, especially in a studio environment. If you don't understand the language you're still in kindergarten. Again, gig lost!

Next, guitarists are guilty of thinking in terms of movable shapes, patterns and grids. Other instrumentalists don't think like that. You might be thinking of a Bb Minor Pentatonic box, but the sax player is thinking 'Bb, Db, Eb, F and Ab'. The fact that guitarists often think about shapes and visual patterns can be great as it does make us play in a unique manner, but if you've ever tried to play something written for a different instrument then you'll already know the notes often don't fit in 'the grid'.

I've regularly found that other instrumentalists have a deeper insight into music, as they deal with the notes on a 'personal' level. They always know which note they're playing, and they never view a note as part of a geometric pattern.

Here's a less obvious point: other musicians often understand rhythm, rhythmic notation and phrasing in a far more intrinsic, internalised way. While guitar tablature can be fantastic for knowing *where* a note is played, it can leave a lot to be desired in terms of telling you *when* it should be played.

Other musicians begin with rhythm and pitch notation being taught by necessity in their first lesson. They don't have handy neck diagrams and shapes to visualise, they just have a pitch and a rhythm to play.

Tablature is useful to quickly communicate an idea, but it's a double-edged sword. Because of our over-reliance on tablature, guitarists quickly fall behind most other musicians in recognition and performance of rhythm and phrasing.

Most recording sessions will involve at least some degree of music reading ability. If the record company is paying thousands of dollars a day for a studio, you'd better be able to play the music right quickly. This might not be as big of an issue as it was 50 years ago, but if you want to get a good reputation as a guitarist, get a good reputation as a reader. There are so few decent reading guitarists it's an easy way to set yourself apart from the pack.

These days, few people will hire you just because you can play 1/32nd note triplets at 140 bpm, but you'll get the gig if you're the only guy in town who can play a written part.

Last, but not least: personal satisfaction. Learning to read music is learning a new language. To be able to turn some black dots and lines on a piece of paper into a beautiful piece of music is one of the most gratifying and special experiences we can have as musicians. Reading music is an achievement that feels fantastic and will stay with you for your whole life.

Real musicians communicate with music notation. It's a little daunting, but it's easier than you think.

What? No Melody!

Most of this book is made up from increasingly difficult lines of pitches and rhythms. I have deliberately written these lines to avoid melodies and tunes as much as possible. The reason for this is deliberate. If the sight-reading examples are written as tunes you will easily memorise them and begin to play them by ear.

Without melody in the exercises, you are *forced* to read each note, rather than letting your ears take over. This keeps your brain engaged, focused and actively involved in recognising each pitch individually. If your brain begins linking a note into a memorable phrase that can be learned as a fingering sequence, the tendency is to stop sight reading and start playing by ear.

Each page of reading focuses on one key and begins by moving between notes that are adjacent. As you descend the page, the examples get more challenging to read because the musical distances between the notes (intervals) gradually increase.

The same idea applies to the rhythm reading exercises in the third section of this book. A new rhythm is introduced (normally every four lines), and gradually combined with increasing numbers of rhythms you have already seen. It may look intimidating on paper, but all the exercises in this book are meticulously planned to challenge you in a constructive, achievable manner.

The idea is to prepare you for anything that may occur in 95% of sight reading examples you may come across in real life. There will always be sight reading challenges out there, but in this book, I aim to get you prepared for what the real world may throw at you in a professional situation.

You may wish to find examples of actual pieces of music to use in conjunction with this book. Violin books are great sources of musical material, and you can even use guitar tab books as most of them contain standard notation. Simply cover up the tablature line with a folded piece of paper.

Get the Audio

The audio files for this book are available to download for free from www.fundamental-changes.com. The link is in the top right-hand corner. Simply select this book title from the drop-down menu and follow the instructions to get the audio.

We recommend that you download the files directly to your computer, not to your tablet, and extract them there before adding them to your media library. You can then put them on your tablet, iPod or burn them to CD. On the download page there is a help PDF and we also provide technical support via the contact form.

For over 350 Free Lessons with Videos Check out:

www.fundamental-changes.com

Over 10,000 fans on Facebook: **FundamentalChangesInGuitar**

Instagram: **FundamentalChanges**

Chapter One: The Three Essential Elements of Reading Music

As complicated as it might seem at first, the process of reading music can be broken down into just three simple elements:

1) Pitch recognition

2) Location of the notes on your instrument

3) Rhythm recognition

One of the reasons that it can be slightly trickier to read music on the guitar is that we have up to six locations to play the same note. The pitch E can be played in the following six places:

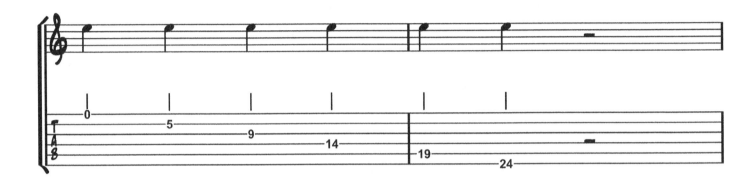

One reason that guitarists stop learning to read music is because of this confusion, but let's look at this logically.

The voicings of the notes in the second bar are probably too high on the neck to be of much use in a 'normal' playing situation, so let's discount these.

The open string has a very specific tone that can sound out of place and unblended in anything other than classical music or acoustic chords.

The voicing on the 4th string is possible, but it's unlikely unless you're already playing in that position on the neck.

The two most likely voicings of the note E occur on the 2nd and 3rd strings. They're also close to each other and not too distinct in terms of tone.

In fact, it is normally true that the best area in which to read on the guitar lies between the 3rd and 10th frets. This is, of course, subjective, but most professional guitarists seem to agree that most music you will come across will normally lie comfortably in this area.

Except for rock guitar solos, I would say this has been my experience of professional reading, and in terms of actual usefulness[1] having knowledge of this range of the fretboard is a high priority.

---

1 No disrespect to rock guitar solos; they're extremely useful but often not notated in a live environment.

While written pitch and rhythmic notation are fairly easy to learn, most guitarists seem to struggle with the application of this information to their instrument.

The notes on the keyboard simply ascend from left to right, but the guitar is less simple. To change the pitch of a note we can either move up the neck or change strings entirely. This three-dimensional aspect to note location can unfortunately stop players in their tracks. However, if we remember that most music is formed from uncomplicated melodies that can easily be shifted around the neck, we start to realise that the guitar neck is a little less daunting than we first imagined.

The first step in learning to read music is always the recognition of a note's pitch on paper, and learning how to transfer it the instrument. When we understand this, we can start to logically approach the task of reading music on guitar.

Pitch Recognition

When we read a word on paper, our brain recognises a pattern and attaches meaning to it. This is a process you began learning when you were a few years old. To be fluent sight readers we need to first recognise the dots and lines of music notation as easily as you are reading these words now. We simply need to attach meaning to new patterns.

Music notation works by giving an almost graphical view of pitch against time. As you read from left to right, this shows time moving forward at a constant pace (governed by *tempo*). The height of the note on the stave (the five horizontal lines) tells us its pitch.

Each line and space is a defined note which will always sound at the same pitch. Here are the notes from the C Major scale with their letter names written in below.

This is a lot absorb, so it is easier to separate the notes on the lines from the notes in the spaces.

The first thing you will notice is that the notes in the spaces spell out the word 'FACE'. This is very handy when we are learning to recognise pitches instantly.

The notes that lie on the lines do not spell out a convenient word. Instead most people use a little phrase to help remember them:

Every **G**ood **B**oy **D**eserves **F**ood.

There are plenty of phrases you can use to remember these notes so try coming up with your own.

Refer back to the scale of C Major and you will see that we haven't covered every note yet but don't worry. It's best to break things up into small steps. Try reading through the following example (without your guitar) to help develop your note recognition skills.

Keep referring to the names previously written if you struggle to remember them.

Now turn to page 30 (the first page of C Major examples) and read the notes along the top line of the page without your guitar. Say each note out loud as you read it. This will reinforce the mental link between the note and your recognition.

This will take time and effort at first, so it is OK to go slowly. When I was learning to read music to a high level, I frequently felt disorientated and hungry when I'd finished, such was the effort it took!

When you have finished reading the top line of page 30 read the top line of page 31. Avoid constantly re-reading the same pieces of music as you'll eventually end up memorising the passage, which isn't helpful.

If you feel ready to move onto the second lines of these pages feel free, but you can get four times the benefit from any line in this book by trying the following ideas:

1) Read it forwards

2) Read it backwards

3) Turn the page upside down and read it forwards

4) Turn the page upside down and read it backwards

Read through the notes on the first line of page 30 using the four methods mentioned above. If you feel confident, move on to read the later lines but there is no need to go too far at this stage.

When you're gaining confidence, set a metronome to 40 beats per minute and say the notes out loud in time with the click. Read two notes for every click of the metronome. Over the period of a few days gradually increase the metronome speed in increments of 5 beats per minute (bpm) to 60bpm or above.

Do all this without your instrument in your hands. Your only job is to memorise the meaning of each dot

Imagine you're an actor and you're trying to memorise your lines without the distraction of having to perform them at the same time.

Now let's extend the *range* of the notes we are reading to cover every note that occurs on pages 30 and 31, both above and below the stave:

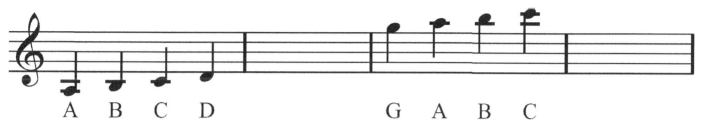

You can now read all the way through these two pages. As this becomes easier, switch things around by using the four techniques above to create new material.

Set the metronome back to 40bpm and work in the same way to incrementally increase your note recognition.

Sharps and Flats

Most, but not all adjacent notes on the stave have an extra pitch contained between them. For example, the note C# (C sharp) lies between C and D. The note C# is referred to as a *chromatic* note.

As you can see, the note C is notated on the stave with a # (sharp) sign before it. I was recently asked in a lesson, "What does hashtag C mean?" I wasn't happy.

For our purposes, the note C# is the same as the note Db (D flat).

The notes C# and Db are referred to as *enharmonic* which is a complex way to say that it is the same note with a different name.

In music, the enharmonic notes are

C# and Db

D# and Eb

F# and Gb

G# and Ab

A# and Bb

They look like this on the stave:

C# Db   D# Eb   F# Gb   G# Ab   A# Bb

Each pair of two notes sounds identical.

Sharps and flats occur regularly in music and are used to either alter a note in the melody, or to designate which *key* we are playing in.

Look at page 54. You can see the sharps occurring frequently throughout the example. When we see a sharp or flat, we play the altered note instead of the original.

Read through the following example:

Instead of saying 'F' in the second bar, say 'F Sharp'. This is the note you would play on your instrument.

Here is an example with a flat (b):

In the first bar, you would say and play the note Bb instead of the note B.

These two examples show how we treat sharps and flats when they crop up in the melody. However, another way sharps and flats are used is to define the musical key of the music.

This isn't a theory book so this explanation will be brief, but by using certain, simple combinations of sharps or flats at the beginning of the piece of music, we can indicate what key the music is in.

For example, by writing an F# at the beginning of the music we define the key as G Major[2]. For more information on how sharps and flats define *key signatures*, check out my book, **The Circle of Fifths for Guitar**.

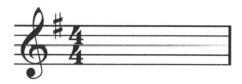

What this means is that *every* time we see an F written in the music, we play an F# instead. This F# is not only played on the specific line it is written on, it affects *every* F in the piece of music unless we're told otherwise.

The notes in the following example are:

F#   C   A   F#   E   F#   C   A   F#

In the following example, all the written B notes are played as Bbs because of the Bb in the key signature.

G   A   Bb   C   Bb   G   E   C   Bb   C   D   E   F

This is the key signature for the key of F Major.

It is essential to take note of the sharps or flats in the key signature and remember to apply them to every note they affect.

Read through pages 44 and 45 remembering to alter the notes as instructed by the key signature.

Don't forget to read backwards and invert the page to create more material to study. The more you do at this stage, the easier you will find it when you apply these notes to the instrument.

---

2   Or E minor, but this isn't important right now.

Work with a metronome to help develop an instantaneous reaction to seeing each dot. Don't worry yourself about the occasional slip up, just try to stay in time and regularly increase the metronome speed slightly.

I advise against practicing sight reading for more than 20 minutes when you are first starting out. Also, practise in the morning before the rest of your practice routine. This kind of work can be quite draining so it is important to approach it when you're fresh.

When you have finished your 20 minutes, take a 10-minute break before picking up your guitar. We have not yet played the written notes on the guitar, but when we do, these same guidelines apply.

Ledger Lines

When the pitch of a note becomes very high or very low it will leave the stave and 'float' above or below it. We have already seen this with the low notes C and D and the high notes G, A, B and C. To help us easily recognise pitches when they are written outside the main stave, we use a system of small lines as a visual reference. These lines are called *ledger* lines. Ledger lines *extend* the range of the musical stave.

Using these ledger lines we can now cover every note on the guitar from the open 6th string, (E) to the 12th fret on the 1st string (also E).

Here are the new notes you need to memorise:

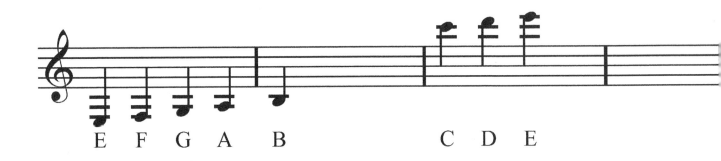

These notes were the ones that took me the longest to develop instant recognition. It may seem silly, but I helped myself with a little rhyme. As the low E is below the third ledger line, I used to say to myself, "Below three equals E." For the top E above the stave, I used to say "Up on three is E."

These little rhymes help a lot as they give you solid reference point from which you can quickly figure out the surrounding pitches. Reading notes on ledger lines is a little harder than reading notes on the main stave, but they are just as important. If you can invent a personal way to memorise these notes you will progress more quickly with your music reading skills.

The electric guitar has a big range compared to many other instruments, and reading ledger lines is just one of the steps we must conquer on our journey to proficiency. If it is any consolation, 80% of the reading you will come across as a guitarist lies between low and high C.

Read through the following examples. Remember you can also read them backwards or invert the page to create new material.

Focus now on page 30 and, beginning on line five, read through each of the examples. Remember to say the name of each note out loud as you read. This is the most important thing you can do to reinforce the link between the notated pitch and your instantaneous recognition.

For the next few days use your 20 minutes of sight reading practice to read out loud the successive exercises beginning from page 30. Remember to include the sharps and flats indicated by the key signatures. Time yourself and work at a speed where you can read consistently with few mistakes. Once again, begin with the metronome set at 40 bpm and read two notes per click.

Don't start from the same place each day. Try to pick up where you left off the previous day or pick a page at random to read. Gradually increase your metronome speed and you will cover more and more ground in each session.

Have patience here: I'm sure you are eager to start applying this information to your guitar (which we will cover in the next section), but I promise you that time spent here will make the task of applying these skills to the guitar much, much easier.

Chapter Two: Playing Written Notes on the Guitar

Once we have begun to develop quick recognition written of musical pitch, the next step is to apply this knowledge to the guitar.

As mentioned in Chapter One, there is normally more than one way to play a single pitch on the guitar. This can be somewhat daunting, leaving us with a nagging sensation of "Am I doing this right?!" The truth is that there are a couple of useful *overlapping* positions on the guitar where it is efficient to read music, but focusing on only one of these at a time is the quickest and most beneficial way to get tangible results.

We will begin by examining where the notes of the C Major scale lie on the guitar. This may not be your favourite shape to use when playing this scale, but it is extremely functional and covers a great range:

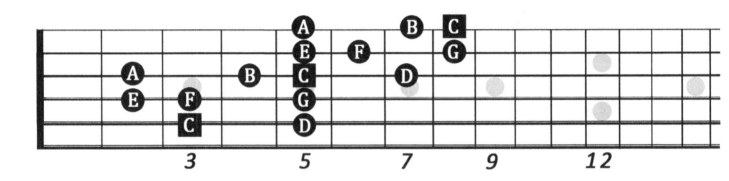

First, become familiar with this scale shape by playing it from low to high.

Hint: begin by playing the lowest C with your second finger. To change position on the 3rd string I normally slide from the note A up to the note B with my first finger.

As you play through the scale, say each pitch out loud.

Splitting the scale into lower and higher octaves, we can now begin to locate the notes on the neck as we read them. Try this example which uses notes in the lower octave:

Say each note out loud as you play it. Reinforcing these links is extremely important.

Now try this example reading in the higher octave of the C Major scale:

C D E G   F A G B   C B F G   F E D C

Here is an example of a melody that moves between the lower and higher octaves of the C Major scale:

E F D C   B A G F   G B C E   F A G C

Of course, this is not the only way to organise the notes on the neck. Try reading through the previous three exercises using this C Major scale shape instead:

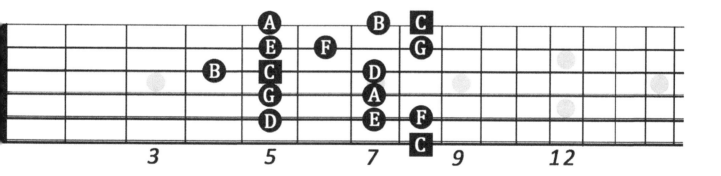

This shape has the advantage of avoiding the position-shift, but it does move us further away from the bass notes on the low E string should we need to play them.

Now move on to playing through the C Major examples on pages 30-31.

Here is a diagram of the locations of the lowest pitches:

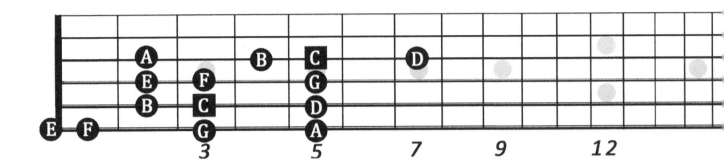

Finally, try using this version of the C Major scale to play through the previous examples and pages 30-31.

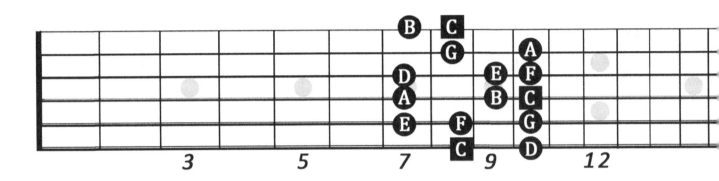

This is a common scale shape and you may already know it. Remember though, you must say the note names out loud as you play them.

Learning the Neck

By splitting the neck into different shapes and areas as you did in the previous section, you will gradually begin to find the strengths and weaknesses of each one.

Remember, the melody of most music is derived from the major scale or one of its modes. By knowing these shapes, we can apply them to any key to give ourselves a huge advantage when we come across new music. We will talk about how to deal with new keys later.

For now, let's look at some very useful patterns that can help us quickly determine the name and location of *any* note on the guitar neck.

Octave patterns are consistent shapes that will reliably tell us how to locate notes of the same name on the guitar. The first thing we must learn is the location of notes on the 6th and 5th strings:

Notes on the 6th string:

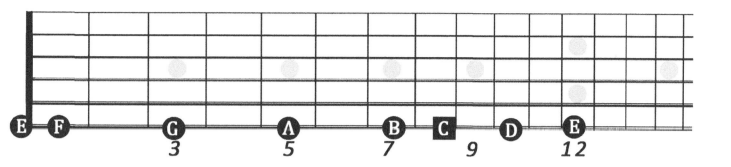

Notes on the 5th string:

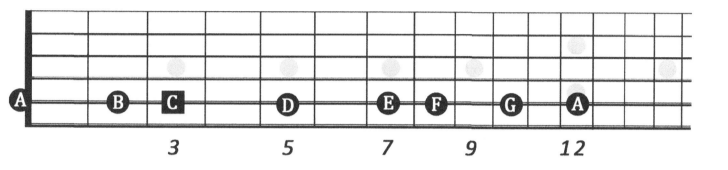

If you already use barre chords in your playing you may well already be familiar with the locations of these notes.

Remember, each note can be adjusted to become a sharp (#) or a flat (b) by shifting it up or down a semitone. Eb and D# are both located on the 5th string, 6th fret or the 6th string, 11th fret.

Now we can use simple shapes to find the same notes in the higher octave.

An octave can be played like this between the 6th and 4th strings, and between the 5th and 3rd strings:

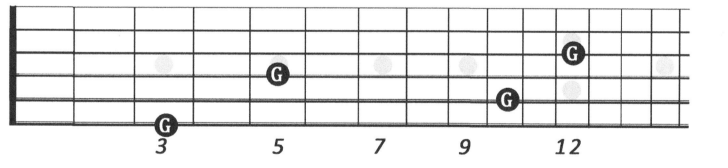

Notice that to play the same note an octave higher you always move *across* two strings and *up* two frets.

Using this information you can quickly figure out all the notes on the 4th and 3rd strings.

You can also play an octave by skipping *two* strings. Here is the octave pattern between the 6th and 3rd strings:

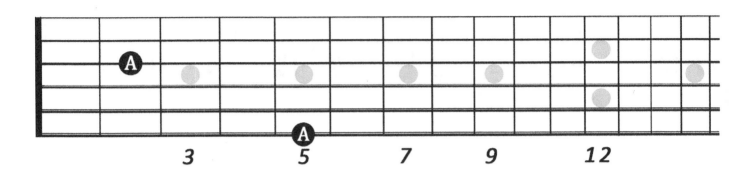

If you know the note name on the 6th string you can locate the same note an octave higher on the 3rd string by moving *across* three strings and *down* three frets.

There is a similar, but slightly different pattern between the 5th and 2nd strings. Because of the tuning idiosyncrasy between the 3rd and 2nd strings on the guitar, the pattern must alter slightly:

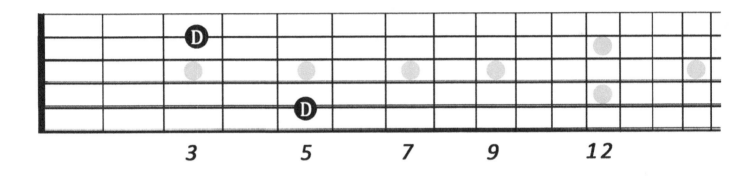

If you know the name of a note on the 5th string, you can locate the same note an octave higher on the 2nd string by moving *across* three strings and *down* two frets.

Between the 4th and 2nd strings, an octave shape will always look like this:

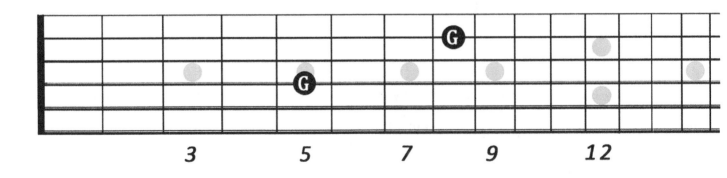

This is identical to the octave pattern between the 3rd and 1st strings:

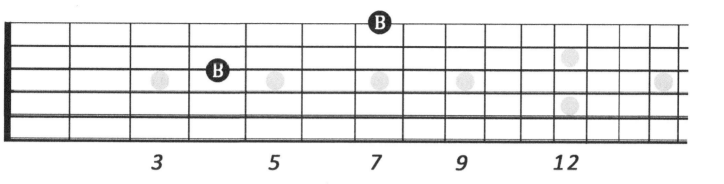

Finally, you may already know that the notes on the 1st string are identical to the notes on the 6th string, just two octaves higher:

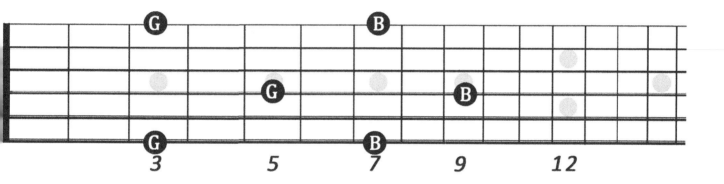

An essential part of learning the neck is developing *instant* recall of these patterns. With practice, the neck seems to get smaller and it takes less and less time to play a musical phrase.

A fun game is to say a note out loud, and then try to find *every* location of that note on the neck as quickly as possible. Don't forget to try this with sharp and flat notes too.

Start by playing slowly through the two G Major pages. Don't forget, every time you see the note F you must remember to sharpen it to F# as shown by the key signature. Use the major scale diagram as a basic structure to help find your note location. Again, every F note needs to be played as an F# by raising it a semitone.

Now read the exercises in the key of F Major on pages 44-45. This time the key signature tells you to play every B note as a Bb. Use the C Major scale shape diagram as a guide to the note locations on the neck, but every time you see the note B, lower it by one semitone so it becomes a Bb.

Reading in Other Major Keys

Sight reading in other keys forces us to incorporate and memorise new note locations on the guitar neck. By gradually increasing the complexity of the key by adding sharps and flats we explore more and more of the fretboard. This in turn makes us more competent readers, and less troubled when we must read unusual melodies.

There are two approaches to learning to read in new keys. We began to explore one of them at the end of the previous section.

Method One:

One way to read in more complex keys is to use the C Major scale as a 'backbone' and adjust the individual notes to take account of the sharps and flats in the key signature. This will quickly improve you as a reader because you are constantly forced to think about the location of the altered notes on the neck.

For example, the act of altering every B to a Bb will quickly teach you the location of all the Bbs on the fretboard. Reading like this is a very cerebral process. It's tiring at first but pays huge dividends in the long run. If you are playing in a key with four sharps or flats you will find you are constantly adjusting your thinking to incorporate these notes.

Remember though, this book is about the *process* of learning to read music. By going through this process now you will learn the guitar neck quickly. After a few weeks or months, you will not be thinking about adjusting the C Major scale to fit the notes in G Major – you will see a notated F# and simply play it without thinking.

Method Two:

The second way to read in more complex keys is to use a fixed major scale shape, and simply translate it up and down the neck into different keys, like you would if you were playing barre chords.

For example, we already know this scale pattern for the C Major scale:

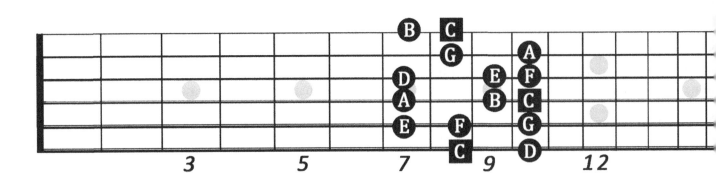

If we wanted to gain quick access to the notes in the key of Bb Major we can shift this pattern down so the root is on the Bb of the 6th string:

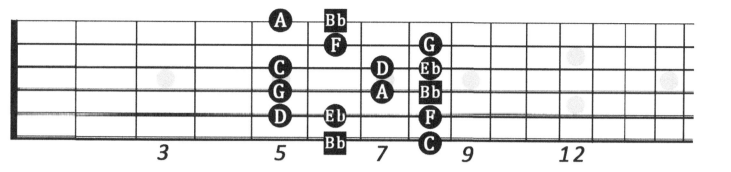

As you can see, we use the same major scale shape in the new position and it automatically incorporates the correct sharps and flats from the new key without a great deal of effort from us as readers.

This is very useful to know, but there are a few drawbacks. First, this shape doesn't necessarily cover the lowest and highest notes in the position. That isn't necessarily a problem, but we may end up having to extend the scale shape lower and higher on the bottom and top strings.

Another issue is that because all the correct notes are automatically provided for us, we will think *less* about the individual pitches being played.

At this early stage in sight reading development, it is beneficial to be working hard to find the notes on the neck and actively thinking about the location of each note.

In real life, the truth lies somewhere in between these two methods. After having worked with method one for a while you will have naturally absorbed the locations of the notes on the neck. As I mentioned, if you see a notated F# you will simply move to the closest F# under your fingers. You will transcend the need to be constantly adjusting the C Major scale and finding pitches will become very easy, if not internalised unconsciously.

It is also useful to know scale shapes, as often in music there are sequential melodies that are much easier to execute when just thinking about patterns.

The only answer is to practice both methods and let them combine naturally in your mind.

Constructive practice and patience is always the key to success. You are learning a new language: this always takes time.

The best ways to practice are detailed on page 27.

Reading in Minor Keys and Accidentals

Fortunately, not all music is written in major keys; about half of the music you will see and hear will be written in a minor key. There are many kinds of minor scales and they all are related strongly to major scales.

Once again, this isn't a theory book, but a brief explanation of the relationship between major and minor scales is appropriate here.

For every major scale, there is a *relative minor* scale that shares the same key signature.

The relative minor scale is always built from the 6th note (or 'degree') of the major scale. For example, the relative minor to C Major is A Minor.

Count up 6 notes from C and we land on A:

1 2 3 4 5 **6**
C D E F G **A**

To form the scale of *A Natural Minor* we simply begin the sequence of notes in C Major again, just starting on the note A:

A B C D E F G A = A Natural Minor

The relative minor to the key of G Major is E Minor:

1 2 3 4 5 **6**
G A B C D **E**

E F# G A B C D

The relative minor to the key of Eb Major is C Minor:

1 2 3 4 5 **6**
Eb F G Ab Bb **C**

C D Eb F G Ab Bb C

These three examples show the natural form of the relative minor. You may also know this scale as the *Aeolian* mode.

This, however, is not the end of the story. The Natural Minor scale is often further altered to form either the *Harmonic* or *Melodic Minor* scales.

The Harmonic Minor Scale

To form the *Harmonic Minor* scale, we raise the 7th note of the Natural Minor scale by a semitone.

For example, we saw that the scale of A Natural Minor was

A B C D E F G A

To change this into the scale of A Harmonic Minor we raise the 7th note, G, by a semitone.

A B C D E F G# A

The scale of E *Natural Minor* was

E F# G A B C D E

Which becomes E *Harmonic Minor* when we raise the 7th degree:

E F# G A B C D# E

C Natural Minor is

C D Eb F G Ab Bb C

C Harmonic Minor is

C D Eb F G Ab B C

The Melodic Minor Scale

The other common minor scale is the *Melodic Minor* scale. There are two forms of this scale, one ascending and one descending. Most modern musicians use the ascending version of this scale, so that will be our focus here.

To form a Melodic Minor scale, we must *raise* both the 6th and 7th notes of the *Natural Minor* scale by a semitone.

For example,

The scale of A Natural Minor (A B C D E F G A), when converted into a Melodic Minor scale becomes:

A B C D E F# G#

E Natural Minor (E F# G A B C D E), converted to E Melodic Minor becomes:

E F# G A B C# D# E

C Natural Minor (C D Eb F G Ab Bb C) becomes:

C D Eb F G A B C

Other sharps and flats introduced into the melody are shown by *accidentals.*

An *accidental* is any note that is altered by a sharp, flat or *natural* in a melody. These accidentals are shown to the left of a notated pitch.

For example, here is the notated scale of E Natural Minor (notice it shares the key signature of G Major).

E NATURAL MINOR

Compare the E Natural Minor scale to the E *Melodic Minor* scale shown here:

E Melodic Minor

As you can see, the 6th and 7th notes are raised to become C# and D# using accidentals.

Here is another example, this time using *naturals*.

Study the notated scale of C Natural Minor (notice it shares the key signature of Eb Major).

C Natural Minor

The 6th and 7th notes in the Natural Minor scale are Ab and Bb, as shown in the key signature. When we raise them in the Melodic Minor scale, we use a natural sign to restore the notes back *up* to the original A and B.

C Melodic Minor

When you sight read new music, you will often see accidentals occur either when the tune contains notes from a minor scale, or when the music changes key (or both).

The following scale diagrams show some useful ways to play the Melodic Minor scale on the guitar in the key of A. These shapes can be shifted into other keys.

A Melodic Minor 1:

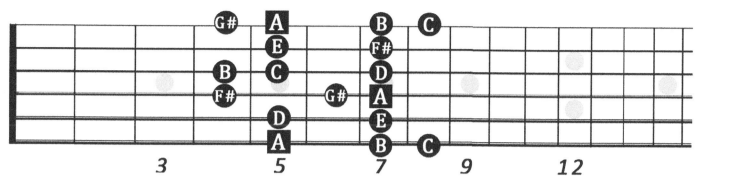

A Melodic Minor 2:

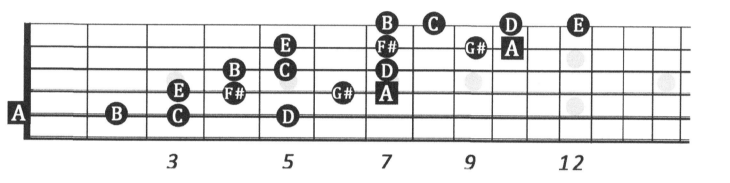

Exercises that use the Melodic Minor scale begin on page 54.

How to Practice the Exercises

The exercises on the following pages are designed to avoid memorable melodies and to gradually increase in difficulty on each line.

The best way I have found to practice sight reading is in short bursts throughout the day, whenever I'm feeling fresh and relaxed. Normally for me this is most mornings and early evenings.

I practise for 23 minutes at a time built from two, 10-minute periods of reading with a 3-minute break where I get up and walk around. Sight reading is fatiguing at first and multiple breaks are essential to keep your brain alert. If you can organise two, 23-minute practice schedules in a day you'll be doing well.

If you have never read before, start with one of the C Major pages and very slowly try to play the pitches on the first line. For now, don't use a metronome. Even if it takes you 10 minutes to do just one or two lines then this is success. Remember to take your breaks and don't do more than 10 minutes reading at a time otherwise you may become tired before practicing the other things you're working on.

After a few days, you will find that you get further down the page in your 10-minute session.

As soon as you feel able (and you don't have to be able to complete a full page before doing this), set a metronome to tick at 50 bpm. Try reading the page again, even if you must read it in 'half time' where each note is held for twice its written value. If you make a mistake, don't stop, just continue and stay in time.

Having the metronome on forces you to recognise notes faster than you would if you were playing freely. This helps the brain develop the instant recognition of language that we require.

When you feel you are getting competent, try reading the second page of C Major notation, but this time begin with the metronome clicking at 50bpm.

Begin to explore key signatures that contain just one sharp or flat (G Major and F Major). Incorporate these into your daily practice routine too. You will soon find that you are able to read two or three pages in a 10-minute sitting. When this happens, gradually increase the metronome speed. First aim to reach 60bpm, then 70bpm and all the way up to 100bpm.

Always ignore mistakes. You'll get them next time! Imagine you're playing on stage and that the band won't stop if you play a wrong note. You just need to stay in time and do the best you can!

Every few days, add a new page of notation beginning with the keys that contain two sharps or flats (D Major and Bb Major), and then three and then four. Hopefully you'll never be in a live situation where you must read a tune with any more than four sharps or flats in the key signature, so fluent reading up to the keys of E Major and Ab Major is a worthy goal.

Incrementally increase your metronome speed. I will often tell my students to do this before they feel ready. Your brain is an incredible thing and can deal with complex information much more quickly than you give it credit for. Even if it feels 'wrong', try upping the speed by a few bpm. You can always slow down again if it is too much.

Don't forget that you can create new melodic material from each line in the following ways:

1) Read it forwards

2) Read it backwards

3) Turn the page upside down and read it forwards

4) Turn the page upside down and read it backwards

When you have spent a few weeks playing through the major key examples, try playing through some of the simpler minor key examples. This will get you used to playing accidentals in written music. Progress through the minor key examples in the same way as you did for the major key examples.

If you are in any doubt about how these exercises should sound, they are all provided on the accompanying audio tracks available for free download from **www.fundamental-changes.com/audio-downloads**

Although the section on rhythm reading is separate from the pitch recognition section of this book, they can and should be worked on in tandem. Flick forward to Chapter Three in this book, and look at the section on rhythm reading now. Find time to incorporate the rhythm reading exercises into your practice routine too.

Melodic Reading Exercises

One of the biggest challenges for new sight readers is the uncertainty that they are playing the notes correctly. For this reason, I have included each example as an audio track for reference.

For every two pages there is one audio track. For example, pages 30 and 31 in C Major are included on audio track #1. There is a one bar-gap between each exercise.

To help you keep your place, there are small drum fills at the end of each four-bar section.

Each exercise is played at 60bpm and may sound quite fast at first. This is to give you something to aim for, but please slow your metronome down to 40 (or even turn it off for a few weeks if you are completely new to sight reading). The sooner you add in the metronome, however, the sooner you will begin to improve quickly.

These exercises are available as a free pdf file from **www.fundamental-changes.com/sightreadingpdf** so you can print them and they will lie flat on your music stand.

C Major

C Major

G MAJOR

G MAJOR

D MAJOR

D Major

A MAJOR

A Major

E Major

E Major

B Major

B Major

F# Major

F MAJOR

F Major

45

Bb Major

Eb Major

Eb Major

Ab Major

Ab Major

Db Major

53

A MINOR

A MINOR

E MINOR

E Minor

B Minor

B Minor

F# MINOR

F# Minor

C# Minor

C# MINOR

D Minor

D Minor

G MINOR

C MINOR

C MINOR

F Minor

F Minor

71

Bb Minor

Bb Minor

Chapter Three: Rhythm Reading

This section of the book is intended to be studied alongside the pitch and notation exercises in the previous chapters. Working on these skills simultaneously will help you progress more quickly.

While the pitch of a note may be learned in isolation and seen as a fixed point in time, melody is always moving forward. It is essential to understand and recognise the most common rhythms that occur in the music we play.

The first thing to realise is that while rhythmic permutations are virtually infinite, there are only a certain number that will be useful for our purposes as modern musicians. This is because only a certain number of rhythms form playable, singable melodies.

Obviously, if you want to sight read the music of Frank Zappa you may well find yourself looking for additional materials to this book (check out *The Frank Zappa Guitar Book* for a truly mind-boggling display of written notation!), but in the following pages I have tried to break down, discuss and illustrate the most commonly occurring rhythms in popular music.

In written music, rhythm is broken down into bars (or measures) and beats.

Bars are containers for the beats. Each beat is named according to how it divides a standard bar of four beats.

For example,

- A whole note fills one whole bar

- A 1/2 note fills half the bar (there are two half notes into one bar)

- There are four 1/4 notes in a bar

- There are eight 1/8th note in a bar

- There are sixteen 1/16th notes in a bar

These notes are written in the following manner:

Underneath each note I have shown its equivalent *rest* value. A rest lasts the same amount of time as a note that has a pitch, but it indicates that there should be silence for the allotted time.

In the UK, there is a different system for naming note lengths:

A whole note = a semibreve

A 1/2 note = a minim

A 1/4 note = a crotchet

A 1/8th note = a quaver

A 1/16th note = a semiquaver

This may seem strange to much of the rest of the world, but our system does have one big advantage compared to the international system: the metric note names of the US system are all based on the premise that there are four beats in every bar.

However, music isn't always written in 4/4 time (four beats in the bar). You can have 3/4 time, 6/8 time or even 17/16 time. In anything other than 4/4 time there are not four 1/4 notes in the bar.

The US system does, however, work very well if we ignore this pedantic fact. It is modern, logical, easier to remember and doesn't involve learning quaint English words!

To begin, clap (or play a muted note) through the following exercise. Set your metronome to 50 bpm and tap your foot on the beat. Tapping your foot is the *biggest* secret to accurate rhythm reading.

Audio example 23:

Note Groupings

1/8th notes and 1/16th notes can be grouped in any mathematical combination as long as we don't exceed a total of four 1/16th notes in a beat. They can be grouped in the following ways:

Audio example 24:

Audio example 25:

Audio example 26:

Tap your foot with a metronome and learn to recognise and *feel* the sound and effect of these rhythms.

Any of the notes in the above examples can be replaced with a corresponding rest value.

Tied Rhythms

It is possible to *tie* two notes together. When you see a tied note, you do not play the second note in the grouping. The first note is held for the value of the second note in addition to its own.

In written music, it is the convention to always leave a space between beats two and three for ease of reading. For example, you shouldn't really see this (although you occasionally will):

The above rhythm should really be written like this:

The previous two examples sound identical; however the second example is written correctly as it uses a tie to clearly show where the middle of the bar is.

If we can show the gap between one beat and another then it is normally easier to read. I would prefer to see this:

Audio example 27:

rather than this:

...because, once again, the gaps between beats are shown. This, however, is a matter of personal preference and the notation shown in the second line is often used.

Try clapping through this example that uses tied 1/16th notes:

Audio example 28:

Dotted Rhythms

You will often see a small dot written after a note. The dot is a rhythmic instruction to *add half of the note value again.*

For example, if we have a note that lasts for 2 beats, and we add half of the original note value again (half of 2 = 1) we end up with a note that lasts three beats.

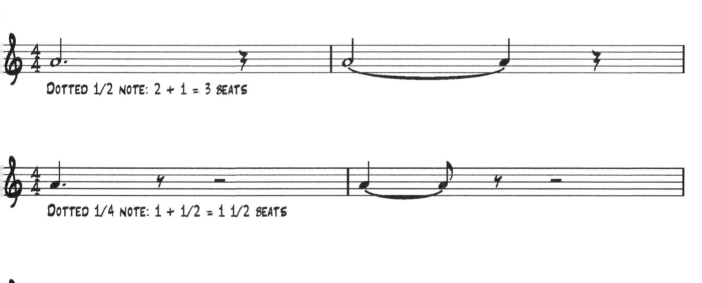

DOTTED 1/2 NOTE: 2 + 1 = 3 BEATS

DOTTED 1/4 NOTE: 1 + 1/2 = 1 1/2 BEATS

DOTTED 1/8TH NOTE: 1/8TH + 1/16TH = 3/16TH NOTES

In each of the above examples you can see how adding a dot to a note value affects its length. In the second bar of each line you can see how adding a dot is mathematically the same as tying the original note to one half of its length.

Normally, the note after the dotted note will make the dotted note 'add up' to a whole number of beats.

For example:

Audio example 29:

1 AND 1/2 BEATS FOLLOWED BY A 1/2 BEAT = 2 FULL BEATS

Audio example 30:

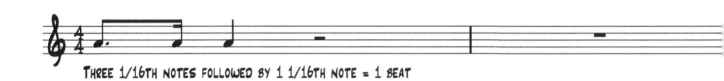

THREE 1/16TH NOTES FOLLOWED BY 1 1/16TH NOTE = 1 BEAT

Triplets

Λ triplet is three notes squeezed evenly into the space of two notes. They are written in a group with the number '3' above them.

When learning 1/8th note triplets it can help to say 'trip-er-let trip-er-let' out loud in time with the metronome. Make sure each 'trip' coincides accurately with the metronome click.

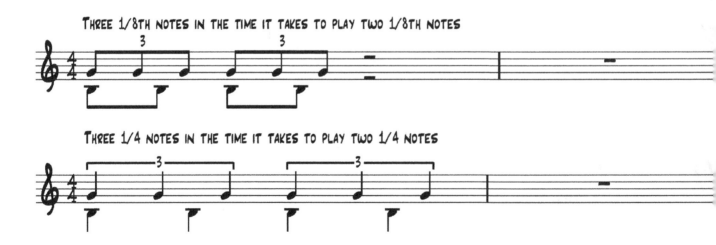

THREE 1/8TH NOTES IN THE TIME IT TAKES TO PLAY TWO 1/8TH NOTES

THREE 1/4 NOTES IN THE TIME IT TAKES TO PLAY TWO 1/4 NOTES

The top line in each example shows the triplet, the bottom line is just there for reference and shows where the original note value lies.

Try clapping through this example. Remember to use a metronome and tap your foot.

Audio example 31:

Any two adjacent triplets can be merged into a single 1/4 note in the grouping. For example, this rhythm forms a basic swing feel:

Audio example 32:

Triplets can also be tied together as you learned in the previous section.

Audio example 33:

Each 1/8th division of the triplet can also be played as two 1/16th notes:

When subdividing 1/8th note triplets into 1/16th notes, you should always feel them as three groups of two.

1/16th Note Triplets

1/16th note triplets are technically when six 1/16th notes are squeezed into the time of four 1/16th notes.

It is, however, normally easier to think of six 1/16th notes in the time of 1 1/4 note.

Audio example 34:

You may be wondering what the difference is between three 1/8th note triplets split into 1/16ths, and six 1/16th note triplets as written above. The difference is in the *phrasing*.

1/8th note triplets split into 1/16ths are phrased as three groups of two (count '1&2&3&').

1/16th note triplets are phrased as two groups of three (count '1&a2&a').

Audio example 35:

If you're struggling to get into the feel of 1/16th note triplets, try saying 'jigery pokery' in time with a slow metronome click.

As with 1/8th note triplets, note divisions inside a group of 1/16th note triplets can be combined. Here are a few examples:

Audio examples 36 and 37:

1/16th note triplet rhythms can be tied or dotted inside the triplets too.

The reading examples on the following pages are organised by note division and each section moves from simple to more complex rhythms as you progress.

Rhythms are written on a single line of notation for ease of reading and to save space. All rhythms are written in 4/4 time.

Approach reading the following pages as you would for the melodic examples in the previous chapters.

Always use a metronome and try to keep your foot tapping in time with the metronome.

Begin with the metronome at around 50 bpm and either clap each rhythm, or pick a muted note on your instrument to play throughout each page.

When you become confident playing the rhythms on just one note, try ascending and descending a scale you know well, while accurately executing the rhythms on each page.

When that becomes easy, try improvising a scalic melody while continuing to play each rhythm.

Finally, write out *one* bar of rhythm that you've been working on, for example:

Apply this rhythm exclusively to one of the melodic example pages in Chapter Two. Stay with the rhythm for the whole page. Make sure the rhythm is written clearly and in view while you're doing this because it will help you associate the written rhythm with the way it sounds.

You don't need your instrument in your hands to practice the following rhythms so they're great to tap out (quietly!) while on the bus or train.

As with any facet of sight reading, you are aiming for instant recognition and application of the notated music. Even though you are learning rhythm and pitch recognition as separate skills, they will quickly combine in your mind and merge surprisingly quickly.

You can hear every exercise on the following pages played as an audio example.

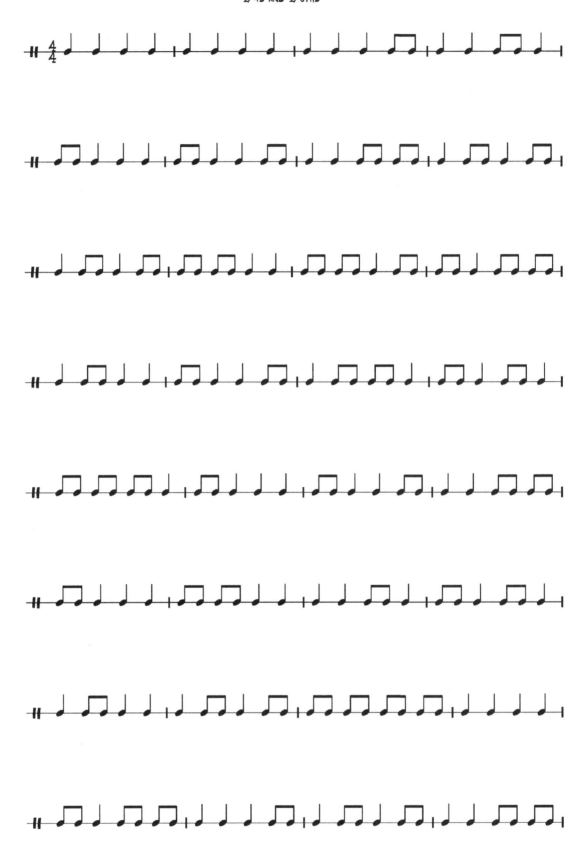

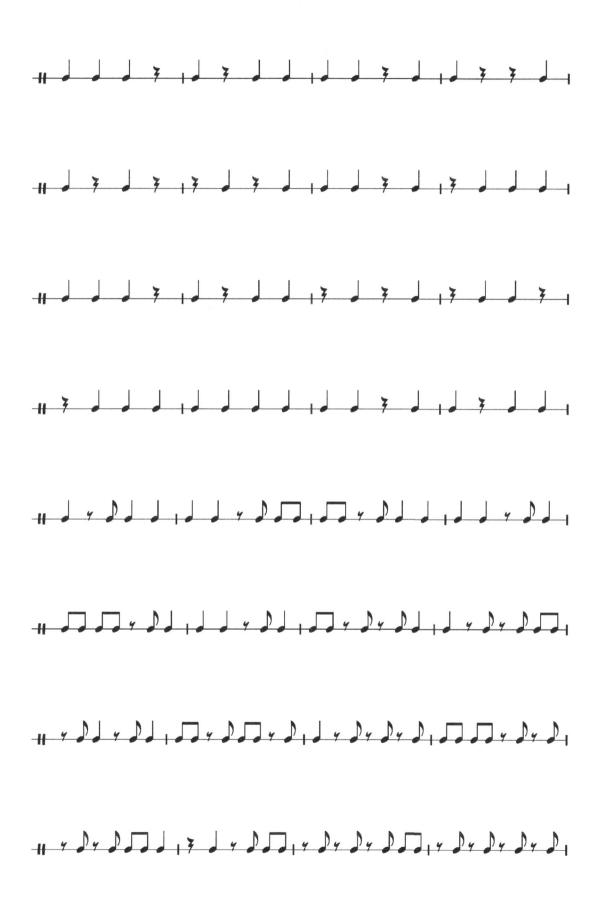

84

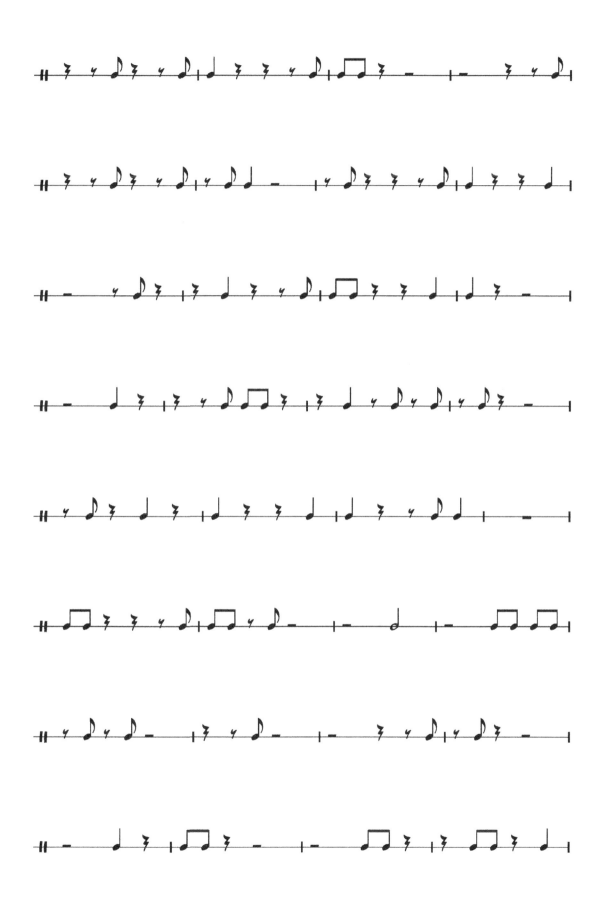

Triplets

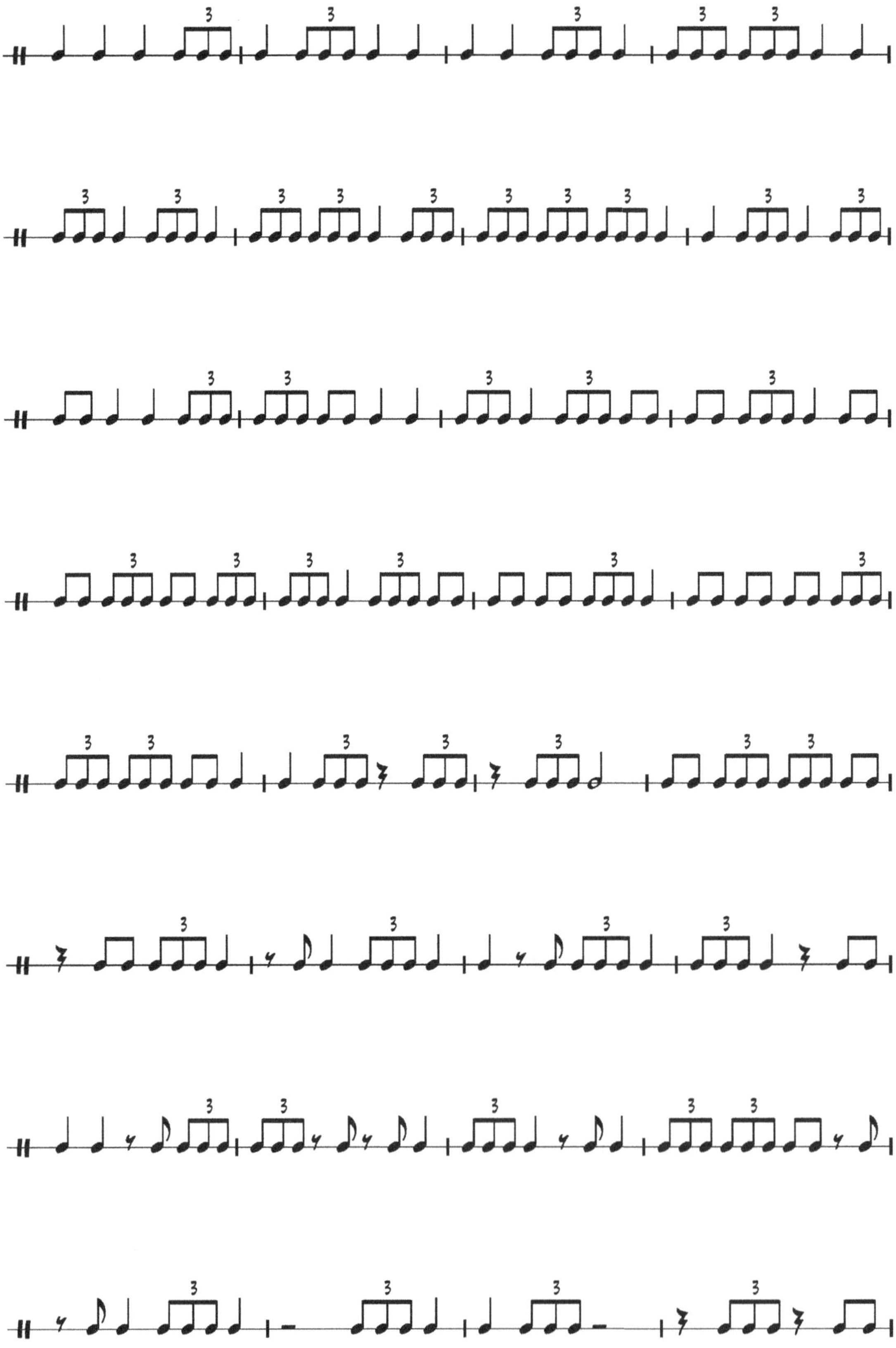

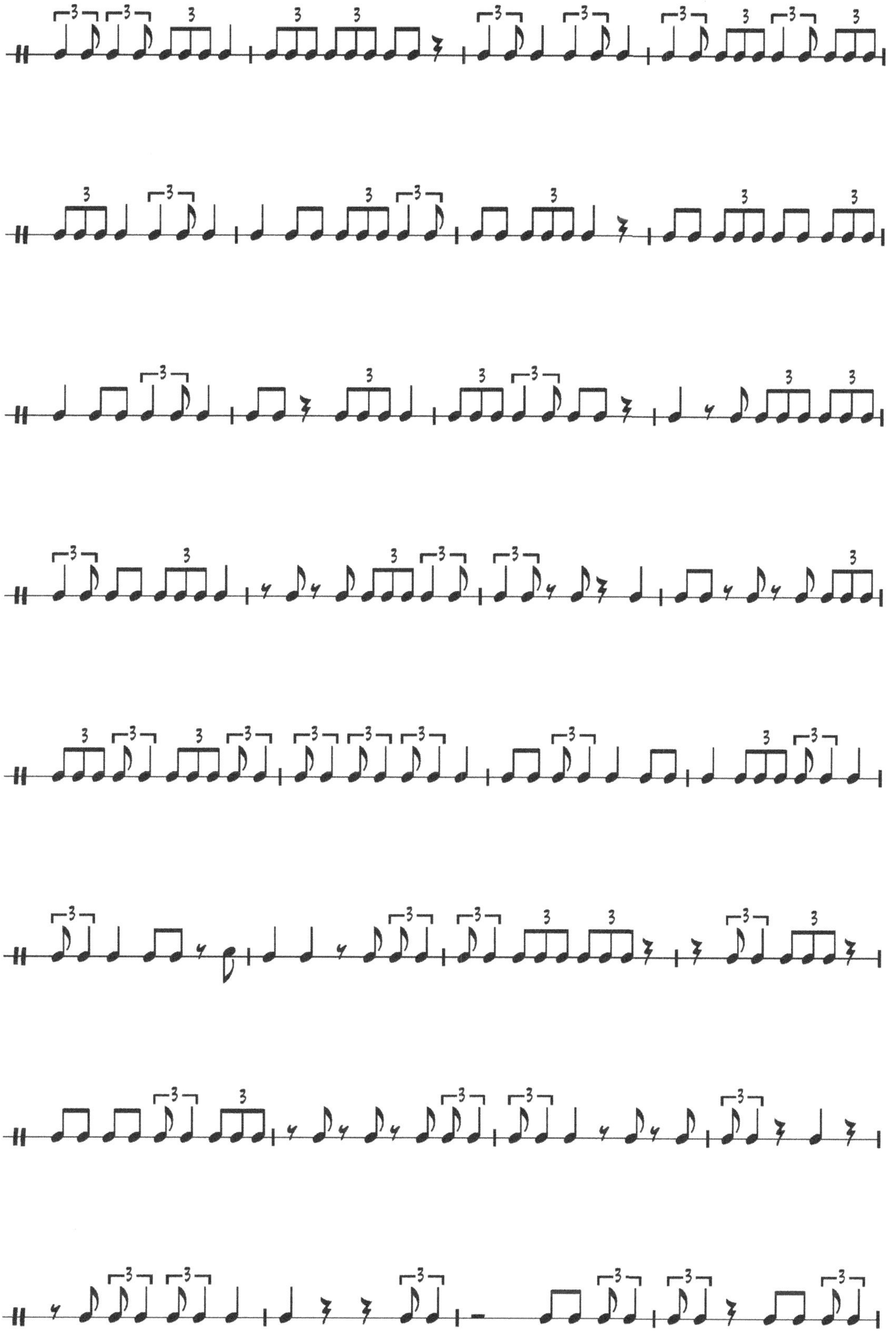

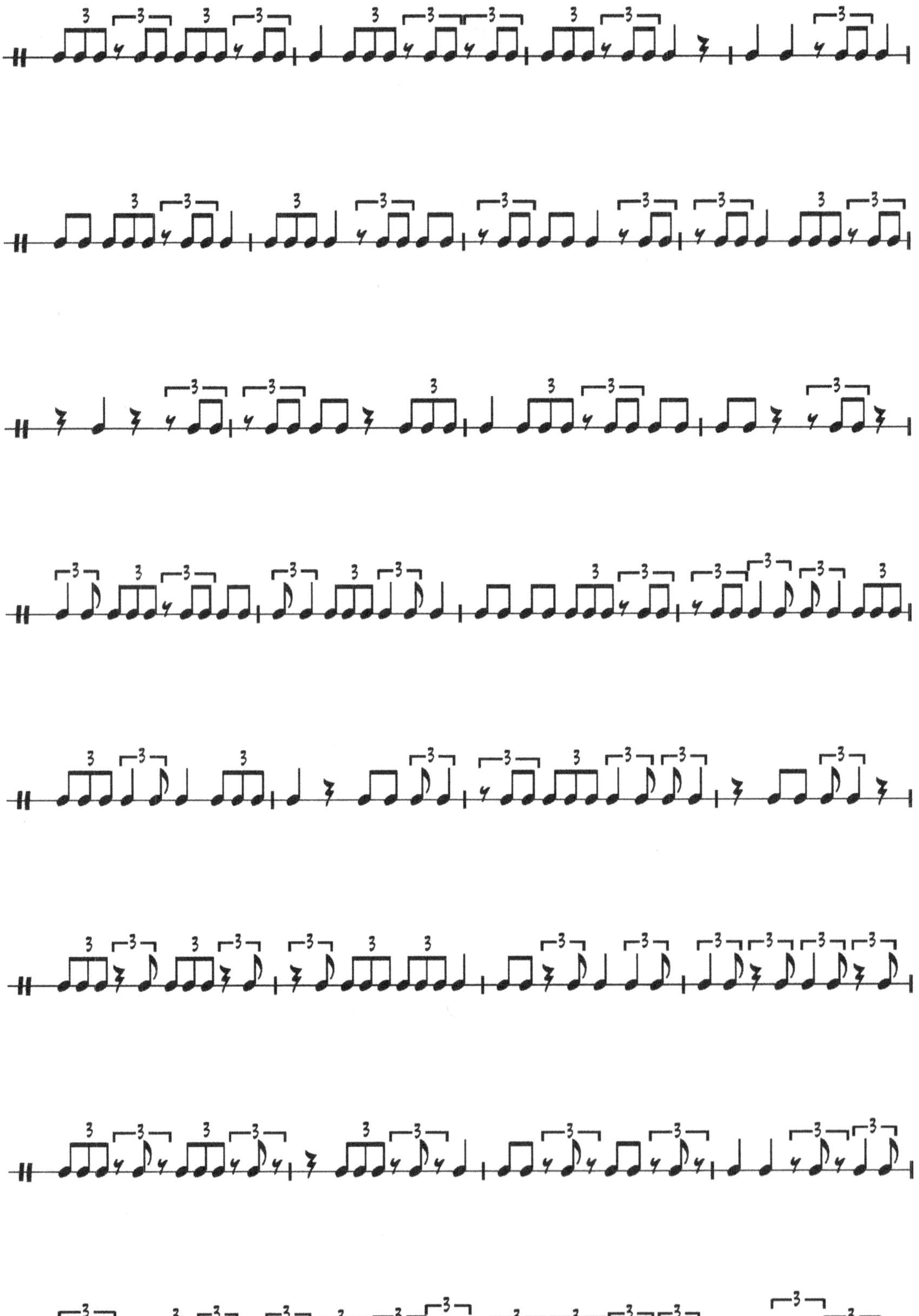

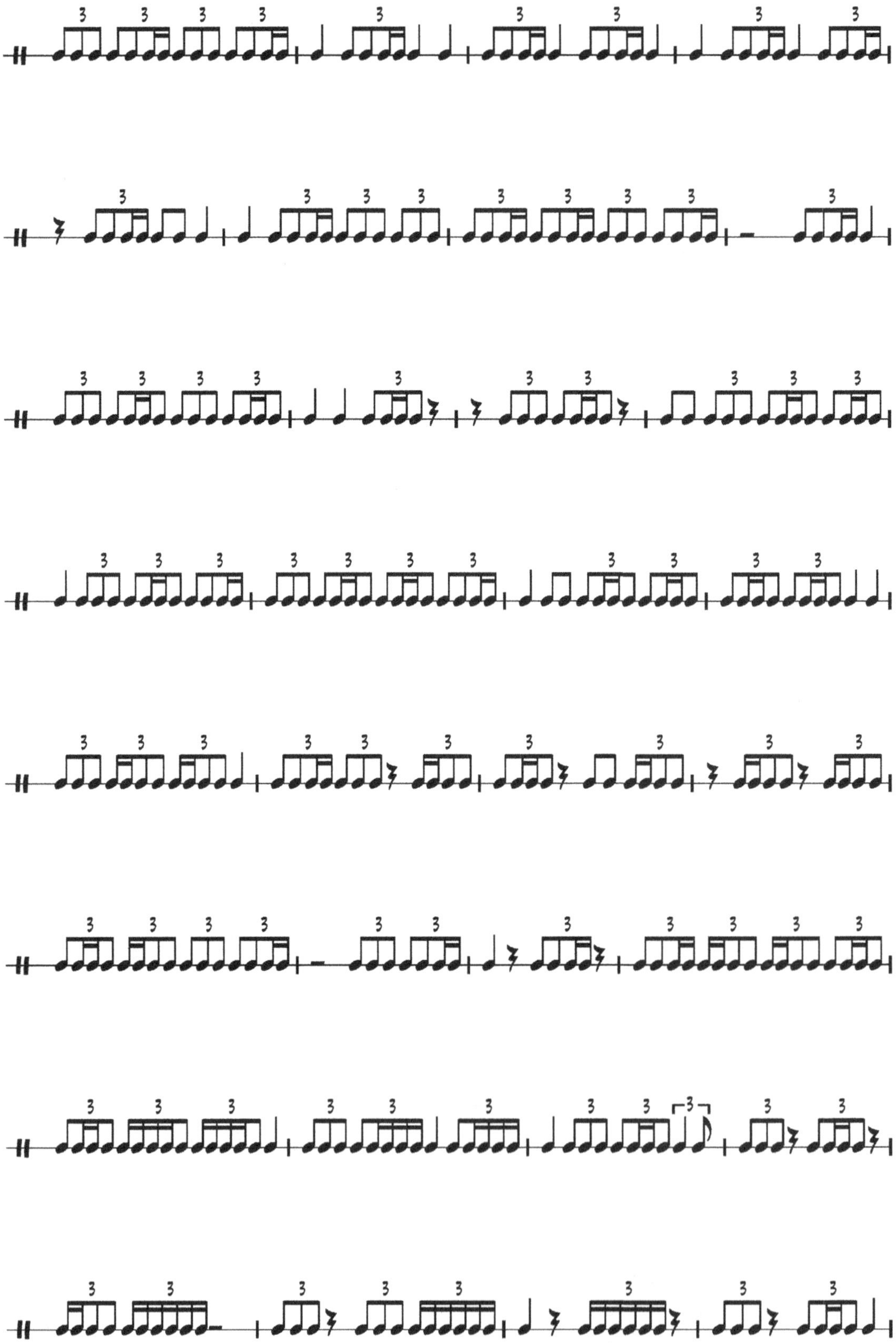

1/16TH NOTES

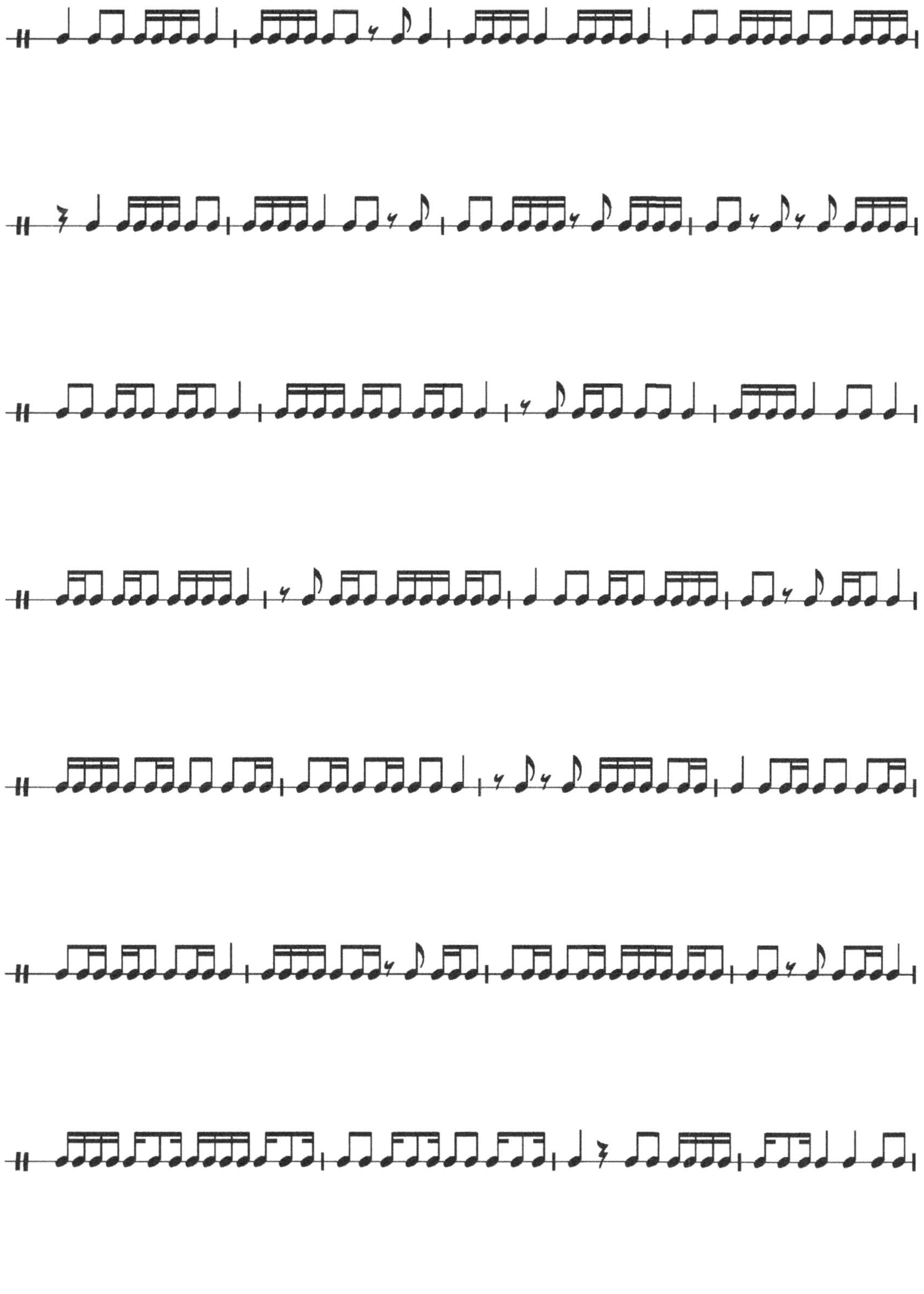

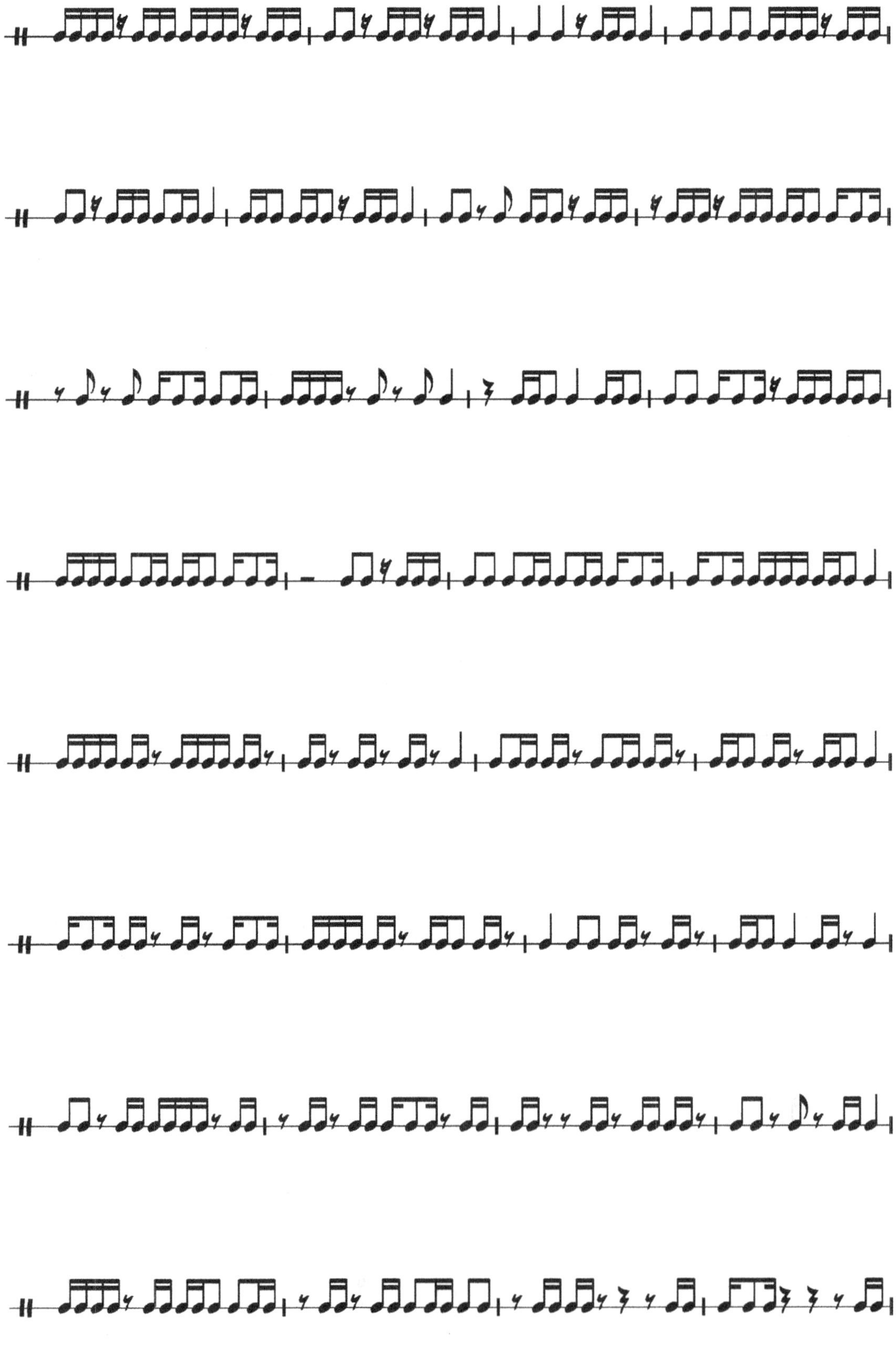

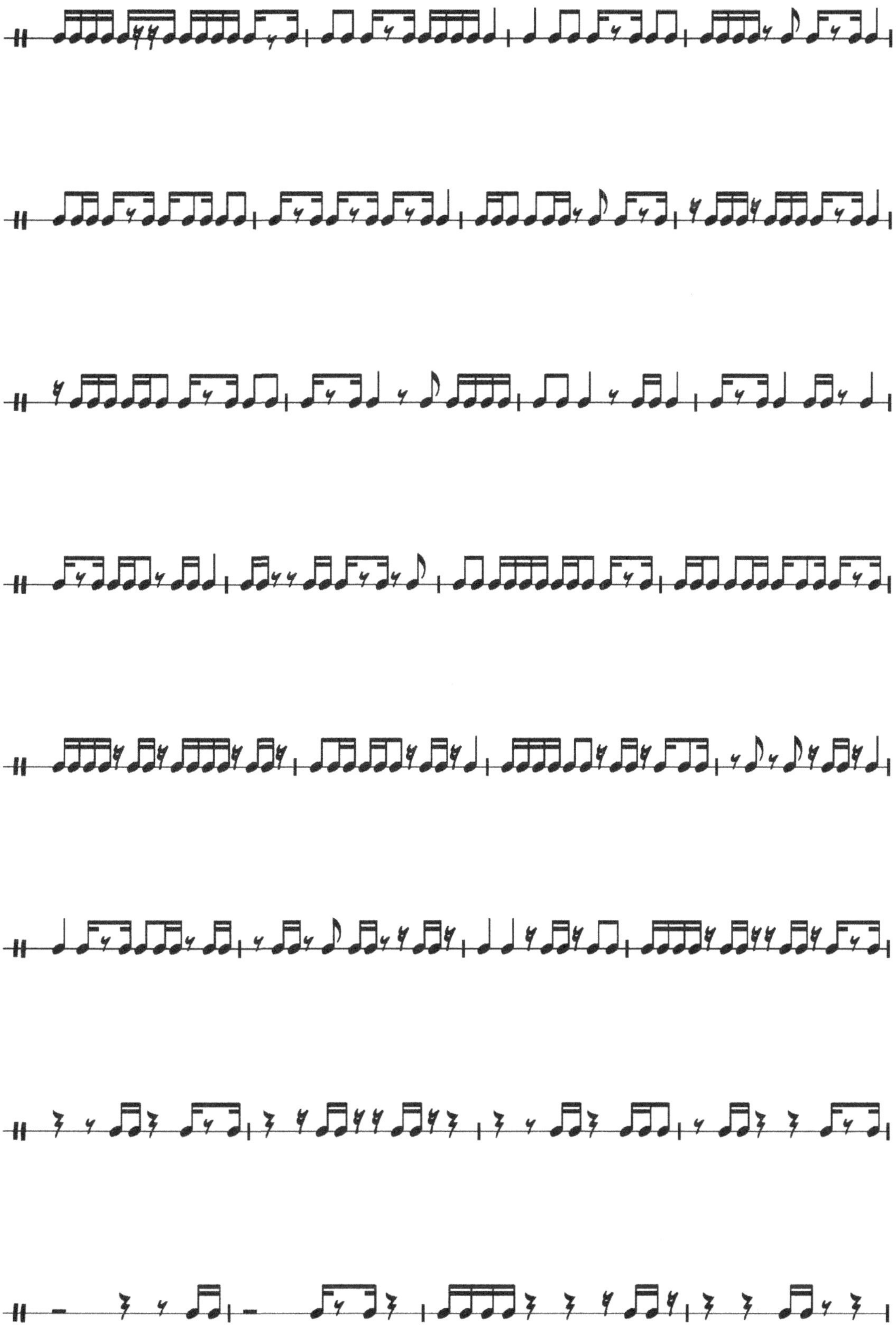

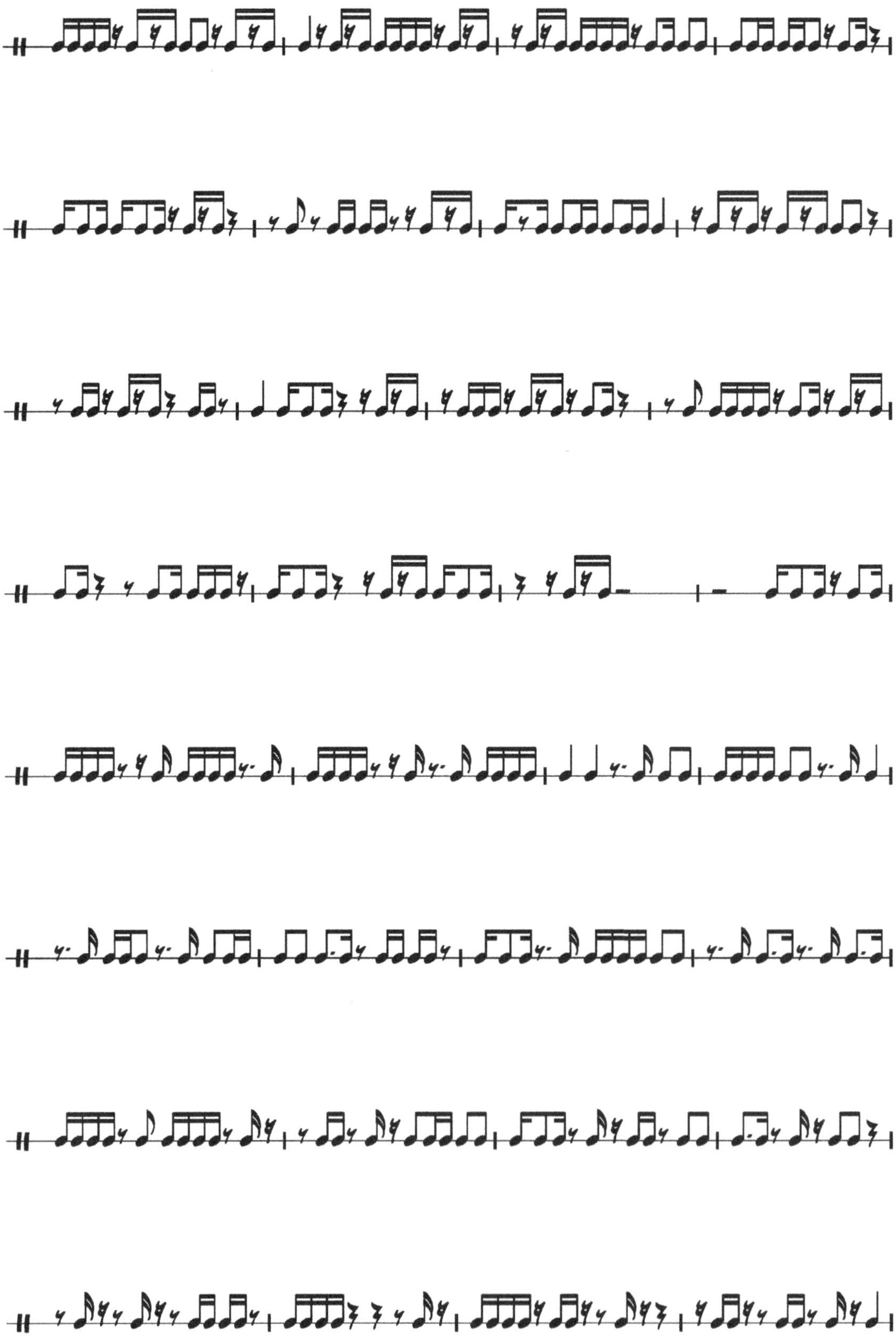

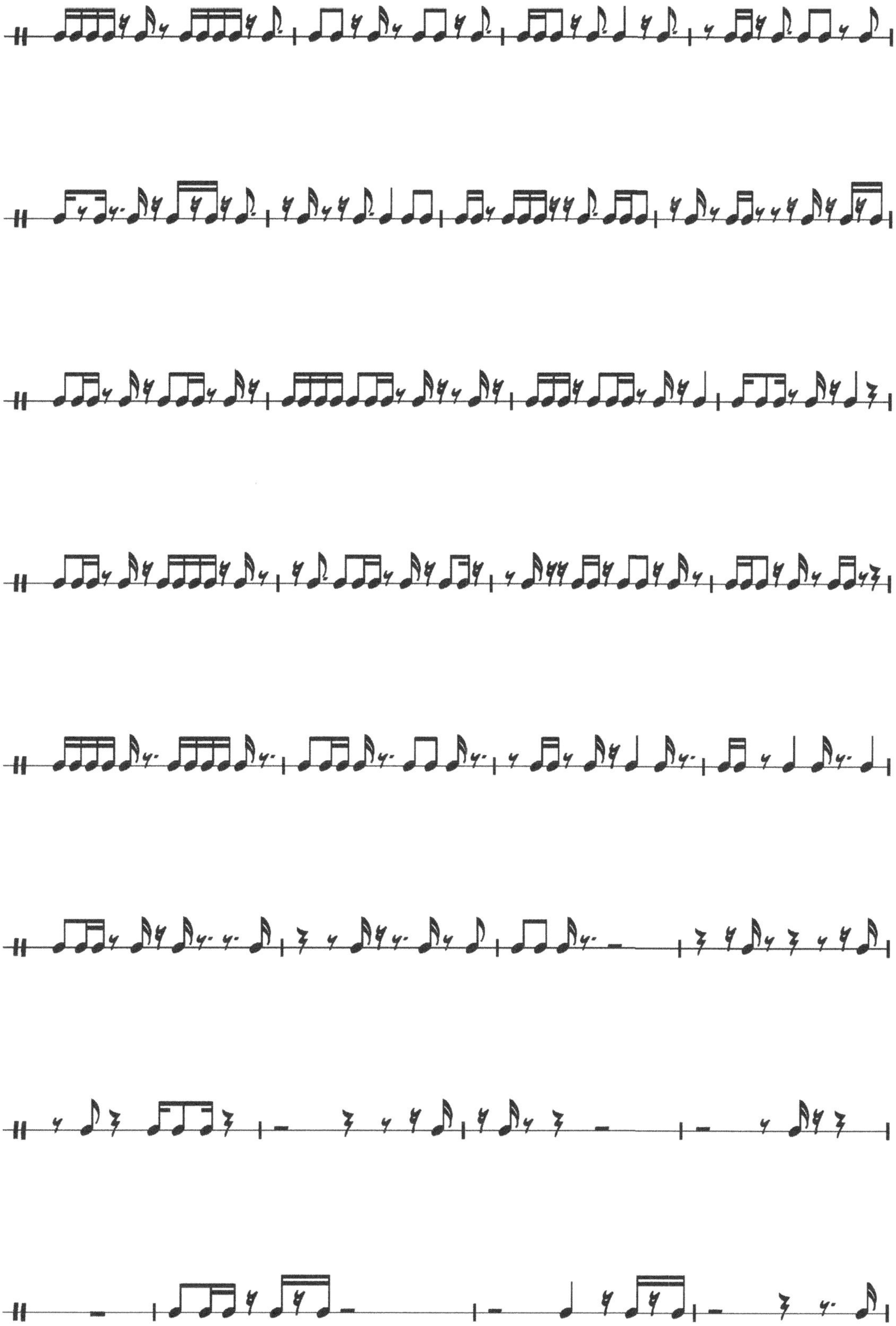

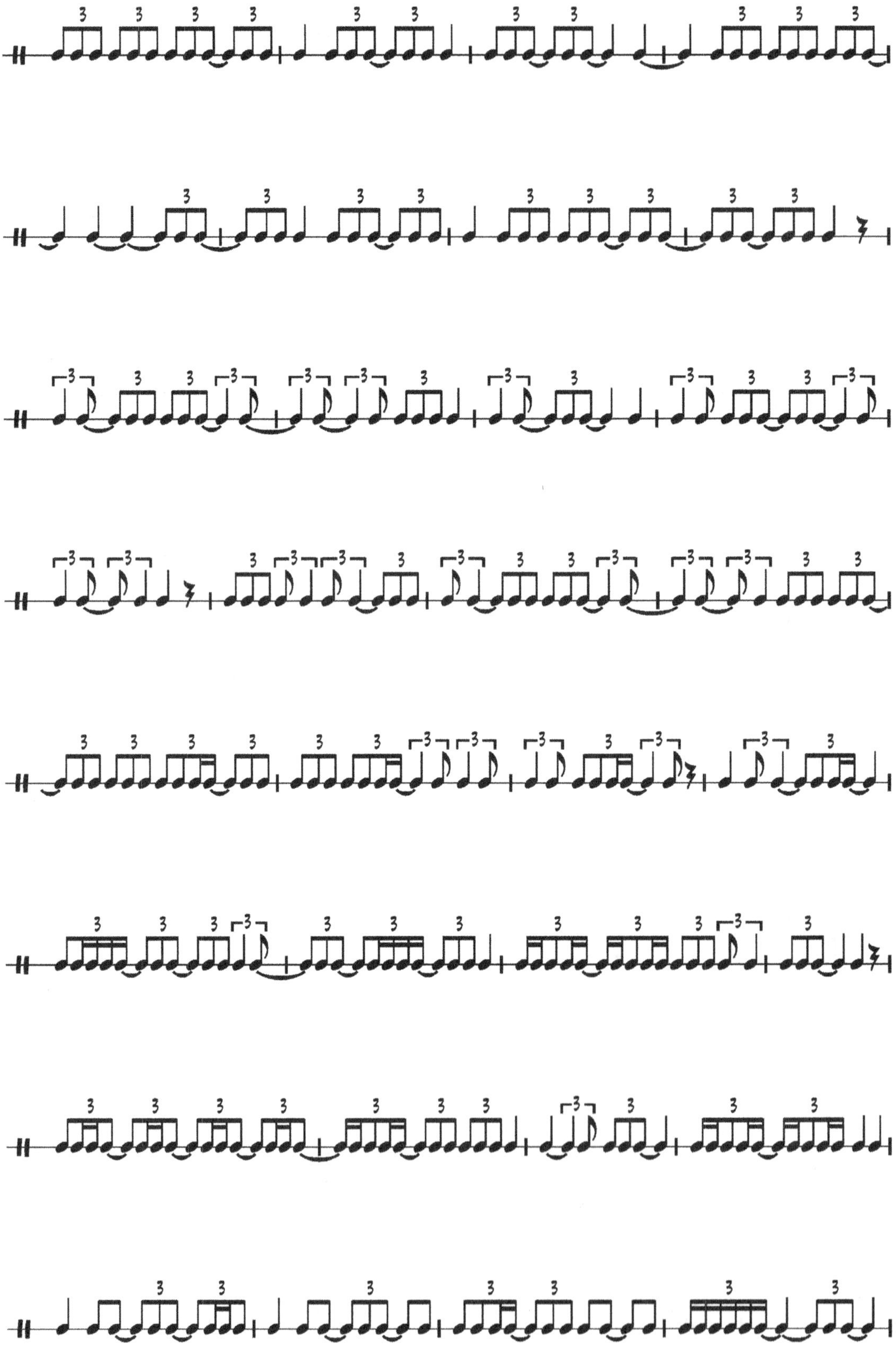

1/16TH NOTE TRIPLETS

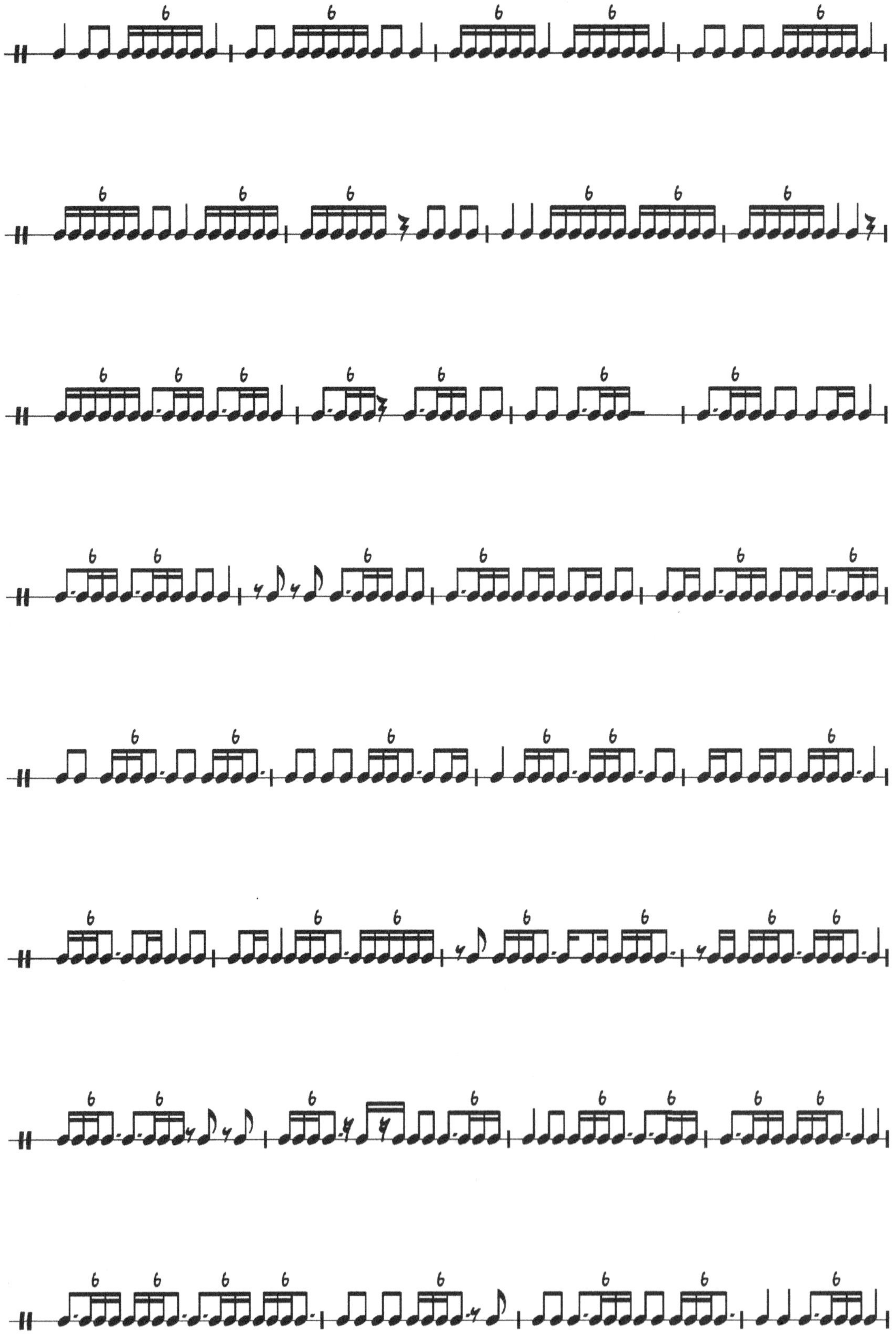

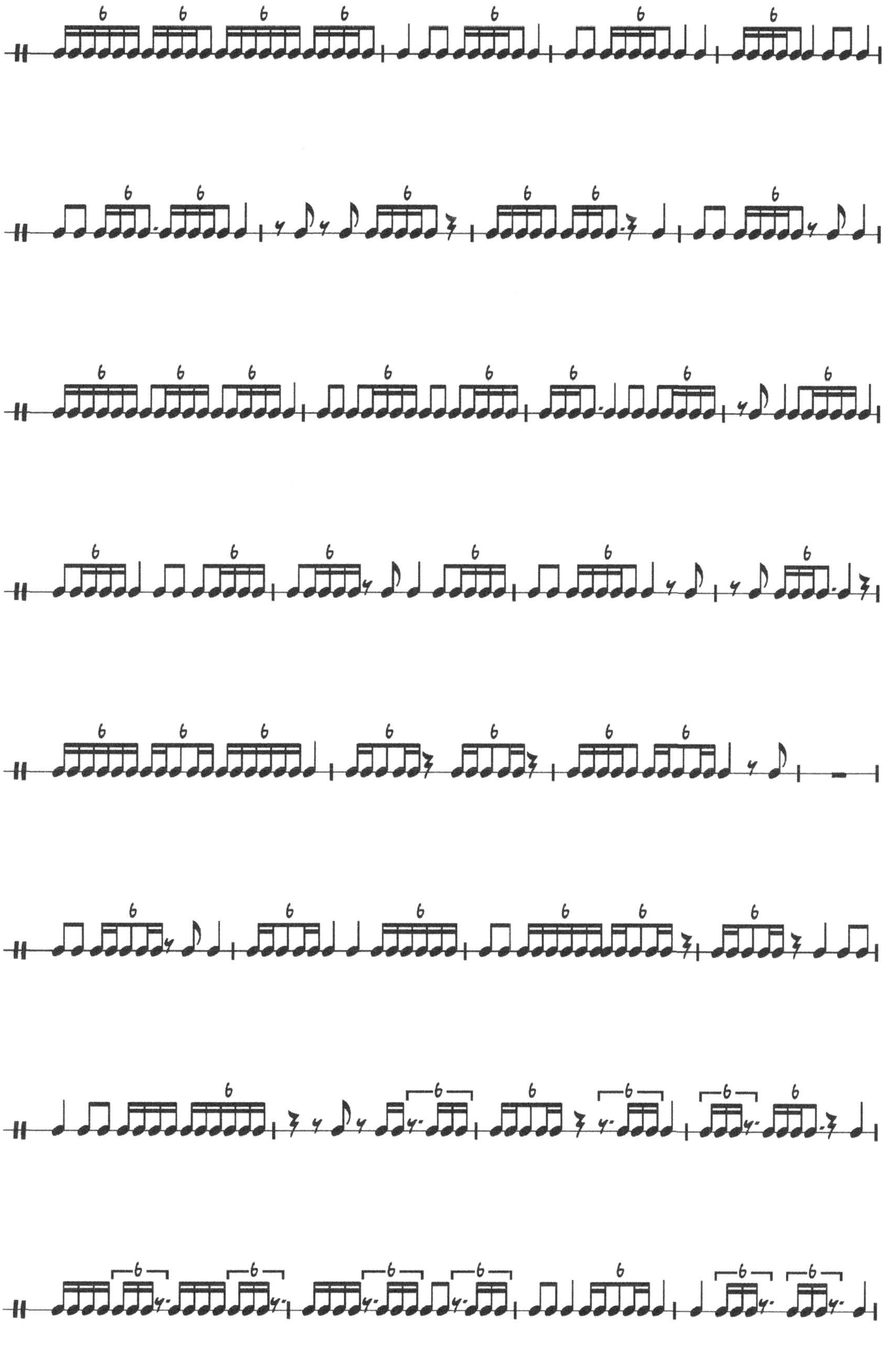
6 6 6 6 6 6 6
6 6 6 6 6
6 6 6 6 6 6 6 6
6 6 6 6 6 6 6
6 6 6 6 6 6 6
6 6 6 6 6 6
6 6 6 6 6
6 6 6 6 6 6

Chapter Four: Time Signatures

Not every piece of music is written in 4/4. Other time signatures have different feels because not only do they have a different number of beats in the bar, the time signature can also imply that each beat is divided up differently.

Earlier, we discussed the difference between the divisions of 1/8th note triplets and 1/16th note triplets.

1/8th note triplets split into 1/16ths are phrased as three groups of two (count '1&2&3&').

1/16th note triplets are phrased as two groups of three (count '1&a2&a').

This grouping makes a huge difference to how the music sounds.

Without listening to examples of different time signatures, it is hard to communicate just how drastically time signatures alter the sound of the music, so as we discuss each time signature I will give you specific musical examples to help you hear the effect of each.

The most common time signatures you will come across are 3/4, 4/4, 6/8 and 12/8.

The top number in a time signature tells us how many beats there are in a bar, but the bottom number tells not only what beat *division* (1/4 notes, 1/8th notes or 1/16th notes) the top number is referring to but also *how those beats are subdivided*.

All the examples in this book so far have been written in 4/4. 4/4 indicates that there are four, 1/4 note (crotchet) beats in each bar.

What is not immediately obvious is the implication of how each beat in the bar should be divided.

If a time signature has a number 4 at the bottom, each beat is normally divided into subdivisions of even groups.

For example:

In the previous example in 4/4 you can see that there are four 1/4 notes in each bar and *also* that each beat is divided into even numbers of subdivisions i.e., twos and fours. You can count 'one and two and three and four and' through any bar of 4/4.

If we want to play any other number of evenly divided rhythms in each beat (3s or 6s) we must use a 'tuplet' (triplets or sextuplets) etc.

A time signature may also imply how each beat is to be *accented*.

Accents are by no means set in stone, but when playing in 4/4 musical convention is that in classical music beats one and three are accented, but in pop and rock music, beats two and four are accented.

A classical example of beats one and three accented in 4/4: **Spring** from **Vivaldi's Four Seasons,**

A modern example of beats two and four accented in 4/4: **Cliffs of Dover** by **Eric Johnson** (and virtually all rock, jazz and pop music).

3/4

The time signature of 3/4 tells us that there are three 1/4 notes (crotchets) in each bar, and each beat is divided into even divisions of two as with 4/4. You can count 'one and two and three and' through any bar of 3/4.

If we wish to play another regular number of notes in each beat (3s or 6s etc.) we must again use a tuplet.

Accents in 3/4 tend to be variable. In classical music there may be a big accent on beat one, but accenting only beats two and three is also common for an 'oom pa pa' effect. 3/4 is often referred to as 'Waltz time', as 99% of waltzes are written in 3/4.

Classical example of 3/4 time: **The Blue Danube Waltz** by **Johann Strauss II**. This is a great example as you can hear how the accents change throughout the piece of music.

Contemporary example of 3/4 time: **Manic Depression** by **Jimi Hendrix** (this is slightly swung, but the 3/4 feel is easy to hear).

After a quick Google search to find other examples of 3/4 time in modern music, it was slightly worrying (and a bit depressing) to find lists of 'modern waltzes' and YouTube 3/4 playlists that contain nothing but songs that are in 4/4 and played as triplets, or simply written in 6/8.

If a piece of music is in 3/4, you can count 'one and two and three and' easily in each bar. If you find yourself counting in groups of three, '123 123 123 123' etc., the music is *either* in 6/8, 12/8 or in 4/4 with each beat divided into triplets.

To clarify this, let's explore the time signature of 6/8.

6/8

When a time signature has an '8' as the bottom number, the common subdivision is 1/8th notes (quavers). However, the important thing is how these 1/8th notes are grouped. If there is a multiple of three as the top number and the bottom number is an 8, then the *1/8th notes are grouped in threes.*

If the 1/8th notes were grouped evenly, then 6/8 would sound identical to 3/4 time.

6/8 indicates that there are six 1/8th notes in each bar and these 1/8th note divisions are grouped into sets of three.

Here is one bar of 6/8:

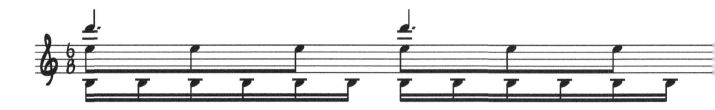

The middle line shows the six 1/8th notes grouped in threes. Because of this there are two main accents in each bar. This is shown on the top line. Each accent is a *dotted* crotchet (three 1/8th notes).

In 6/8 there are two main accents in each bar and each accent is split into three subdivisions.

This should highlight the difference between 3/4 and 6/8:

In 3/4 there are three accents divided into twos. In 6/8 there are two accents divided into threes.

6/8 has a bouncy feel to it, it is the time signature of most Irish jigs and most nursery rhymes.

There are many classical examples of 6/8 time, but one I particularly like is **Chopin's Ballade No 2**.

A very clear, more modern example of 6/8 time is Queen's **We are the Champions**.

Also check out **When a Man Loves a Woman** by Percy Sledge.

Interestingly, I had to listen very carefully to *When a Man Loves a Woman* before deciding to include it in this section.

With many 6/8 songs, it can sometimes be ambiguous as to whether the music is written in 6/8 or 12/8. My feeling is that *When a Man Loves a Woman* is written in 6/8 because the chord changes every two beats (one bar of 6/8), but it could be written in 12/8 with two chords per bar. Let's explore how this ambiguity can arise by examining 12/8.

12/8

The time signature of 12/8 implies that there are four main beats in the bar and, each beat is divided into three 1/8th notes in the following way:

One bar of 12/8 is theoretically identical to two bars of 6/8. In other words, it can be hard to distinguish between the following two examples just by listening:

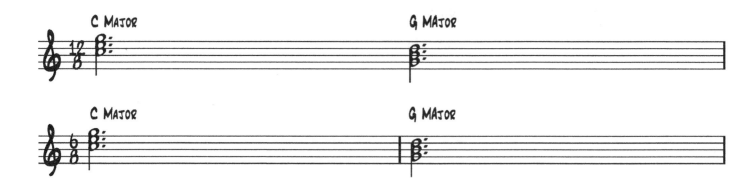

The difference between these examples is normally more obvious in rock and pop music because of the different accents in the drum beat.

These two drum patterns – one in 12/8 and one in 4/4 – will also sound very similar, if not identical:

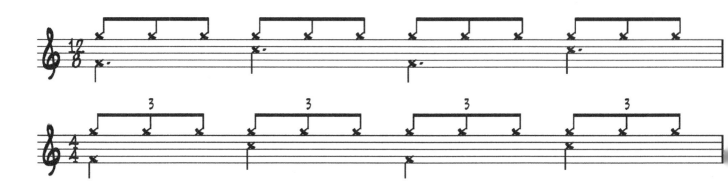

This is a book about sight reading and so recognising the differences between key signatures and knowing how to phrase the music within them is important. In the previous example, I know I'd prefer to be reading the top line because it looks a lot simpler on paper.

There *are* some very subtle rhythmic differences between playing 6/8 and 12/8 but they mainly boil down to different musicians' perceptions of where the accents should be. Also, the phrase length of the melody can sometimes give us a clue.

For now, keep focused on the fundamental skills of pitch recognition, location on your instrument and rhythm reading.

Conclusions and Further Study

This book has covered the skills you need to become an excellent sight reader. It is a long journey, and one that you will always have to make room for in your practice routine if you are to become truly proficient.

The material in this book is designed to last you for years. Don't forget the tricks of reading a line backwards and turning the page upside down to create new material for yourself. If you really run out of ideas, try reading a page as if it were in a different key. For example, pick a page in D Major and pretend it is in Bb.

The key to learning to read music instantly is consistent practice and not being afraid to increase the metronome speed.

The truth is that the best readers in the business aren't really sight reading anymore – they have simply done so much practice, and have so much experience, that they've seen everything before. This is the way you read written words now after having practised your whole life.

When you see a new or complex word in a book, you have mastered the mental process of breaking it down into recognisable syllables and piecing it back together so it makes sense almost instantly. This can be the case when we're sight reading. 99% of the music can be perfectly readable, but there may be one phrase that troubles us.

In the few minutes you have before playing the music for the first time, scan the manuscript for these phrases, and spend the time you have figuring out first the rhythm, and then the pitches and locations of the notes on your instrument.

If you have got to the stage where you unconsciously know the notes on the guitar, and have instant recognition of notes on the stave, I can almost guarantee that it would have to be a very unusual rhythm that will trip you up.

Written musical pitches and note locations on the guitar are finite, but there are virtually limitless permutations of rhythms. Fortunately, most music is formed from similar groups of rhythms, and this book has covered most eventualities.

Finding New Material to Read

One of the advantages of the 'random note' approach to the pitch exercises earlier in this book is that they're extremely hard to memorise. One problem with traditional reading books is that once you have read through a musical example a few times, it will tend to stick in your head and you will begin to play by ear.

This means that you're not really sight reading anymore and this can reduce the effectiveness and life-span of sight reading books.

If you're simply looking for new material to read, and you're not too bothered about the style of the music, I would highly recommend reading classical violin and flute scores for practice. An abundance of classical music has been written for these instruments over the past few hundred years and it easy to source for free on the Internet.

One fantastic resource is **http://www.freegigmusic.com/** where there are hundreds of pieces of classical music freely available. You can search by instrument or even extract the parts from an ensemble.

There are plenty of websites offering PDFs of out of copyright classical music, so spend some time searching and you will always manage to locate some great stuff.

There are some wonderful sight reading books whose names come up repeatedly, one of the best being *For Guitar Players Only* by Tommy Tedesco.

Other popular texts that I have worked with are

- *Modern Reading Text in 4/4 For All Instruments* by Louis Bellson

- *Odd Time Reading Text For All Instruments* by Louis Bellson

- *Reading Studies for Guitar: Positions One Through Seven* by William Leavitt

- *Melodic Rhythms for Guitar* by William Leavitt

- *Advanced Reading Studies for Guitar* by William Leavitt

These are all excellent resources, but they all generally give the same advice that I will repeat here:

1) Practise in short bursts

2) Use a metronome

3) Don't stop playing! Rhythm inaccuracy is normally more noticeable than melodic inaccuracy

4) Have fun!

Good luck with your reading studies. I hope this book helps you to quickly reach your sight reading goals.

Joseph

For over 350 Free Guitar Lessons with Videos Check out:

www.fundamental-changes.com

Twitter: @guitar_joseph

FB: **FundamentalChangesInGuitar**

Instagram: **FundamentalChanges**

Made in the USA
Las Vegas, NV
03 February 2025

17444796R00059